UNLEASHING THE IMAGE OF GOD

DISCOVERING YOUR IDENTITY, PURPOSE, VOCATION, AND CHARACTER

PERRY L. GLANZER

Baker Academic
a division of Baker Publishing Group
Grand Rapids, Michigan

Published by Baker Academic
a division of Baker Publishing Group
Grand Rapids, Michigan
BakerAcademic.com

Printed in the United States of America

Library of Congress Cataloging-in-Publication Data

Names: Glanzer, Perry L. (Perry Lynn) author
Title: Unleashing the image of God : discovering your identity, purpose, vocation, and character / Perry L. Glanzer.
Description: Grand Rapids, Michigan : Baker Academic, a division of Baker Publishing Group, [2026] | Includes bibliographical references and index.
Identifiers: LCCN 2026003180 | ISBN 9781540969040 paper | ISBN 9781493456031 ebook | ISBN 9781493456048 pdf
Subjects: LCSH: Theological anthropology—Christianity | Image of God | Identity (Psychology)—Religious aspects—Christianity
Classification: LCC BT701.3 .G58 2026
LC record available at https://lccn.loc.gov/2026003180

Some names and details have been changed to protect the privacy of the individuals involved.

Cover design by Chris Kuhatschek

Baker Publishing Group publications use paper produced from sustainable forestry practices and postconsumer waste whenever possible.

26 27 28 29 30 31 32 7 6 5 4 3 2 1

"The idea that we are made in God's image is not new, but it is too easily reduced to a background cliché. This engaging book invites you to the realization that by embracing your identity as God's image bearer, you are not just recognizing your profound worth and that of those around you. You are joining a story deep and wide enough to bring empowering meaning to your work, your play, your values, your very self."

—**David I. Smith**, Kuyers Institute for Christian Teaching and Learning, Calvin University

"All humans must deal with the basic question of who we are. While mature Christians have learned to use the reality of our status as image bearers to shape our self-identity, college students are in the middle of trying to find those answers. Fortunately, Perry Glanzer is able to mix his empirical analysis with biblical wisdom to create a valuable guide to help Christian students think about these issues. This book will be useful for Christian students, and it also has a postscript that will be insightful for those who work with students, such as staff and professors."

—**George Yancey**, Baylor University

"This book is a beautiful gift that college students and their parents and educators so desperately need right now. Perry Glanzer's argument is simple, yet the implications are anything but that: To succeed in college and in life, students need something greater than academic efforts and professional aspirations. They need to know that they are beloved persons made in God's image—and this knowledge will change everything. This is the gospel, and in our age of chaos, stress, and ever-encroaching AI, we need to hear this truth, for it will set us free."

—**Nadya Williams**, books editor, *Mere Orthodoxy*; interim director, MFA in Creative Writing, Ashland University

"Perry Glanzer has spent his career reflecting on the implications of the creation narrative for the identities that college students are called to navigate, discern, and embrace. These pages now bring to bear those years of reflection, inviting students to chart pathways of faithful discipleship. Anyone invested in the future of students would also be well served by considering these reflections and acting as inspired. In a world growing only more disorienting, such a book is a testament to the hope Christ-animated learning offers the next generation."

—**Todd C. Ream**, Indiana Wesleyan University

To the image of the invisible God

Contents

Acknowledgments

I am grateful to the many previous Christian scholars who contributed to unpacking what it means to be made in the image of God. They first built on God's foundation, and I hope merely to expand on that work. I am also grateful to all the administrators, faculty, staff, and students whom I have interviewed during my career. They are the ones whose voices shared how central understanding the image of God was in their lives, which motivated me to author this book. Finally, I also want to thank Jessica Martin and Austin Smith for their invaluable editorial work and comments on previous versions of this book. They saved me from numerous errors.

Introduction

Erin appeared to embody the model college student success story.[1] As a minority student who overcame an extremely difficult family background to attend an Ivy League institution, she saw herself as someone who set goals and achieved them. However, she confessed a weakness: "I'm the kind of person that if I don't have some sort of an end goal, it's just really hard for me to motivate myself to do anything."

In high school, she had goals and the support needed to reach them. She recalled, "I just kind of chugged through high school, you know, you have more of a structure, and it was easier." After Erin came to college, however, she shared that the adjustment was more difficult than she thought it would be. She confessed, "I don't think I ever completely adjusted." She soon realized that the problems she faced were multifaceted: "Socially, it was difficult because there was so much competition. Academically, it was difficult just because the level, the standard, was much higher. . . . Psychologically, I think I was still dealing with my family stuff."

The "family stuff" pertained to how her dad had left home when she was in sixth grade. The result was that she closed herself off to supportive relationships: "That was when I felt that I needed to be independent in order to survive. I can't rely on my family. I can't rely on my friends. . . . I just ended up really isolating myself." Erin realized that her parents' divorce

1. All names of students in this book are either researcher- or participant-chosen pseudonyms.

had shattered the illusion of safety and support she once had. Therefore, since her earthly father proved unreliable, she decided to rely completely on herself.

The final result of all this turmoil and her attempt to rely more on herself was paralysis, or what Erin described as "no sense of motivation, no sense of what I wanted to study, and I had no interest in going to class, and so I ended up saying, 'Okay I can't do this.'" Suddenly, she found that she could not even rely on herself.

She admitted the core of the problem was a lack of any sense of worth and purpose, which manifested itself in different ways: "I was struggling with an eating disorder throughout high school, and so that had been getting serious—and I think that's also linked with a lack of a sense of meaning." Unfortunately, Erin did not find help from her university at that time, and she eventually spiraled into depression. As a result, "I took that year off to recover from my eating disorder and my depression and to search for a sense of meaning."

Erin struggled with something that everyone must face at some time in their lives. For the first eighteen years of our lives, we rely on our parents, teachers, and other adults to structure and coauthor our lives. By coauthor, I mean that we derive our conception of who we are and who we should become from others and the groups they have created. Our parents guide us, and school provides a structure and a set of goals.

Still, at some point, your parents cannot, and should not, be the primary coauthors of your life, and the structure of the K–12 school disappears. Like everyone else, you will eventually leave your old high school friends and the social identities you've built in that context. You may no longer be able to identify as an honors student, a basketball player, a member of the band, or a member of a particular student group.

At that point, you must face a couple of key questions and choices: (1) To what degree will I choose to "self-author" my life—and thus my worth, purpose, and character—or continue to coauthor my life but in new ways? By self-author, I mean that you choose your own identities of importance and the purpose and goals for your life. (2) What will motivate me and provide me with a larger identity, a source of worth, a purpose, and a motivation to grow in character? The answers you discover to these questions make all the difference in the world for your flourishing, the flourishing of those around you, and the world's flourishing. There are two paths to follow.

Discovering Your True Self Versus Being a Fake

We all despise being around phonies. Parents concerned about cussing often despise one of the great works of adolescent literature, *The Catcher in the Rye*, because it constantly drops F-bombs. Yet the most important F-bombs to pay attention to in this novel are a different four-letter word beginning with *F*: *fake*. The main theme throughout the book is that the young adult protagonist, Holden Caulfield, is frustrated with the people around him, whom he considers to be living lives of inauthenticity. All of us, but especially young emerging adults, possess an ardent desire to avoid people who are "fake."

The problem we all face, though, is that it is hard to be authentic if you have no idea who you are. Furthermore, becoming someone you are not leads to living an inauthentic or fake life. You will wind up going through life taking off and putting on masks to try to play a part that has nothing to do with who you really are. Indeed, humans can become quite adept at putting on and removing masks, depending on the crowd. But trying to be someone you are not remains one of the most despairing, inauthentic, and destructive approaches to life.

If this journey is your experience, you might feel as though life has become an awkward performance through which you stumble, hoping never to be exposed as the fake you are. You spend your life trying to please others, but it is never enough. As a result, you may lack worth, confidence, a sense of belonging, a personal purpose, and deep-rooted character. Most of all, you will lack an understanding of your core identity.

That is not to say that we do not have some hint of our core identity as we choose to live the life of the phony, the fake, or—to use biblical language—the hypocrite. For example, when we interviewed Maria, she was recovering from losing her true self. As with many young college students, she had started college trying to make friends by experimenting with various identities.

She shared that, unfortunately, the journey did not go as she had planned: "I had a very toxic friend group freshman year, and I very much became someone *that is not myself*, which is somebody who would go out every weekend and party and drink a lot and do things that I hated, but I still did, because that was the environment that I put myself in" (emphasis added). As a first-year student searching for friends, she had become someone she did not think she was, due to the need to find belonging and acceptance in a group. In this scenario, she saw herself as a hypocrite.

Interestingly, she had also placed herself in another environment, one that created a war within herself regarding who she should be: "You know, I would still go every Tuesday and Thursday to my Religious Hour choir rehearsal. One of the biggest moral dilemmas that I had was that of living the life of a hypocrite—the life that I wanted to live versus the life that I was living. And what had hit me was just a really terrible night. I went out when I really should not have, the first time I ever blacked out. I hate it. I hate that. It makes me cringe thinking about it because it's the worst." Maria recalled that she had let herself become someone she had never wanted to be.

Fortunately for her, the other community in which she had placed herself extended a transformative grace she never forgot: "The next morning I had to drive to Houston with my choir to sing at a nursing home and lead worship at some churches in Houston. And I was hungover, and I was throwing up on the side of the road. And these people were nothing but kind to me. And I didn't tell anybody why except for one person." Maria's identity conflict is one experienced by humans everywhere. We tend to think of ourselves as having a "true core self" and then also a self that is influenced by social contexts.

Usually, we think of our true core self as fundamentally good, but we also find ourselves becoming what we do not want to become (e.g., Paul's experience in Rom. 7). When I served on my university's honor council committee, we would constantly hear students talk about how the cheating in which these students engaged "was not really me." Why do we think that way at times? Are we simply deceiving ourselves? Or are we harkening to a lost identity that we do not know how to recover and live out?

This book argues that the central problems facing young, emerging adults—indeed, anyone of any age—stem from a core problem. We do not know who we are, but we do have a longing for a good, purer self we somehow lost. Although the first two chapters address the consequences of this core problem, this book will focus the bulk of its attention on what it means to discover our whole and coherent true self—the self gifted to us by God. Knowing this self helps us understand who we are and how to flourish as human beings.

Said differently, the primary purpose of this book is to unpack the implications of what it means to be made in God's image and how to fully bear God's image in our lives. Christians usually know that sin has chained and enslaved the God-given desires from our original identity as image bearers, turning them to serve other masters. Thus, through Christ we must unleash our original identity as image bearers and fulfill our original design. Still, we often do not understand the specifics of what that might entail for key issues related to human flourishing, such as self-worth, belonging, purpose, and character development.

During my college years, I would have benefited from the kind of insight and mentorship I am hoping to offer within these pages. As a Christian father and educator, I feel compelled to share with you what I have learned in my years of studying and researching moral and faith development in college students. Thus, I draw on the Christian intellectual tradition and the latest contemporary research to guide our path toward greater flourishing. I am writing this book to serve young emerging adults, many of whom are in college—and the church more broadly—by exploring, and making more accessible, a biblical understanding of God's ultimate purposes for our lives, the process of owning those purposes, and the ordering of our loves in the face of competing purposes. In other words, I will explore the biblical and social science resources that describe the intellectual tools necessary for being and bearing God's image.

Road Map for the Book

I start in part 1 by explaining the core problem with how universities approach identity and who we should become. Emerging adults are subjected to a buffet of possible selves by which they might determine what is "good." Society encourages us to think of ourselves as either individual self-authors or members of a particular social, gender, or racial tribe; citizens of a particular nation-state; romantic lovers; and other identities deemed important at the university. Of course, all these identities are important, but understanding yourself primarily according to one of these stories distorts the worth, motivations, and character qualities you believe you must acquire to fulfill your purpose. We need a better foundation.

Part 2 introduces this foundation. It explores the first practical ramification of what it means to understand our identity as image bearers of God: Our worth comes from being made in God's image. In other words, moral motivation must start with an understanding of our value that is not contingent on our performance. This beginning requires a level and type of humility that may run contrary to the intellectual confidence students are expected to develop in college. In contrast, we must recognize our intrinsic value as image bearers of God.

It then proceeds to explore how, through Christ, God has restored the image we have defaced. God not only provides a way to restore this image but also gives us a new identity and mission. He gives us a new motivation for recovering God's image that springs from our response to his loving actions. Furthermore, through Christ, God gives us a clear understanding of what it means to bear God's image. We must know, love, and acquire God's virtue to become who God made us to be.

Part 3 demonstrates the incredible impact that an understanding of the doctrine of the image of God has had on human history. This doctrine provided the basis for elevating the dignity of the poor, women, and the mentally and physically handicapped. It also served as the foundation for arguments against slavery and the mistreatment of Native Americans. Likewise, this doctrine served as the basis for expanding the vision of various forms of education and including every type of person in this vision.

Part 4 explores the practical contemporary implications of understanding ourselves as created in God's image. It examines what happens when we recognize this as the source of our worth. Moreover, God not only made us in his image but also designed us so that we might grow further into that image. Unfortunately, sin has caused us to seek human flourishing apart from this design. Thus, the basic pattern one sees in both the Hebrew Scriptures and the New Testament is that God acts to redeem and reconcile to himself the alienated creation that he has made in his image. This reconciliation occurred through Christ, the true image of God, and it provides a new motivation, springing from gratitude, to recover and live out what it means to bear God's image. Christ also provided new power, through the Holy Spirit, to know, love, and acquire God's virtue—the ultimate goal for image bearers.

Part 4 concludes by explaining that bearing God's image involves demonstrating his virtues in the context of multiple human identities. In other words, just as we know God through his different identities (e.g., King, Lord, Father, Shepherd, Potter, Friend, Lover), and God is excellent in these identities, so we too are called to be excellent in our different identities. For example, we are to love God, our family, our neighbors, and yes, our enemies. We are to show kindness, forgiveness, and justice in the same way that God is kind, forgiving, and just. Furthermore, part of our motivation to acquire and demonstrate these virtues stems from the fact that God has designed us to bear his image, and one of the ways we do that is by acquiring and demonstrating God's character in these different identity contexts.

I end the book with one final practical application and a postscript for professors, administrators, and student life staff.

PART I

Navigating the Buffet of Identities

Trying to Find Yourself in College

For the first eighteen years of your life, you have people telling you who you are. You enter a world with a name bestowed by your parents. God gifts you a sex, and society defines your ethnic or racial identity for you. You grow up in a country, region, state, and city you did not choose, or, like me, multiple regions, states, and cities you did not choose. You are required to attend various institutions where your identity is defined for you. Scholars and marketers give you a generational name (Gen Z, etc.). You join some endeavors based on your interests (e.g., basketball, band, art), but the identity and standards of excellence for such endeavors were established long before your time. Other people and institutions are largely defining who you are and what you should do.

When you leave home for college or work after high school, though, these older identities become causes for intellectual exploration, notice, and/or struggle (member of a particular ethnic or racial group, man or woman, citizen of a specific geographical location, Christian, agnostic, neighbor, child of divorced parents or a single mother, etc.). Yet you also suddenly find yourself less bound by certain parental expectations and the identities you inhabited in high school. That freedom opens new opportunities to experiment.

You may have previous identities gathered in high school that you happily or unhappily discard (nerd, band member, outsider, athlete, member of a certain club or clique, etc.) that are now replaced with other identities (college student, technical worker, blue-collar worker). Suddenly, a greater degree of choice regarding your identity opens up. You can choose student groups to join, you can choose your future professional identity (e.g., accountant, engineer, social worker, teacher), and in most cases, you can choose your romantic partner. You can choose your worldview (Christian, atheist, Buddhist, etc.), your political identity (conservative, liberal, Democrat, Republican), and many other identities.

Considering this reality, it is no surprise that when I ask students about the purpose of college, one of the top answers they give is that it is a time to discover who they are, as the quotes below illustrate:

- "So, it's a place where you develop values and figure out more about your own identity, especially leaving high school and leaving your parents' house. It's a place you find yourself and decide what you want to do in the future."
- "The purpose of college is definitely to figure out who you are and get yourself out of the structure that you had while you were being raised, which kind of dictates what type of person you can be by what your parents believe. And in college, it's all you deciding what you want to do . . . it's just a big discovery period."
- "I definitely think it is to find myself."

So, how do students find themselves in college? And on what identity do they build their sense of worth? That's the subject of chapter 1. In my research, I find that students primarily socially author or self-author their lives. Unfortunately, those approaches lead to some deep-rooted problems. Chapter 2 sets forth how our problematic understanding of ourselves can negatively influence our purpose. Chapters 3 and 4 then set forth a Christian alternative that not only addresses these problems but is rooted in reality not in one's own or others' creation.

CHAPTER ONE

The First Problem with Losing Yourself

Losing Your Worth

I feel like I find worth in relationships, which I know can be risky. They go wrong too.

—Soren, American college student

Being recognized for my accomplishments is definitely one thing that makes me valuable. I know that that's probably not the best thing to make me feel recognized and valuable. But I feel like that's human nature.

—Tucker, American college student

Susan was an eighteen-year-old first-year student at a large public university when our research team conducted an interview with her. Although she would later identify as a Christian in our interview, she answered most of our questions without reference to her faith. For example, when we asked her what gives her worth, she shared, "My friends, really. I feel like I picked the good ones, you know? They always support me and tell me how good I am." Susan also added that her value comes from her brother and parents. She derived worth from "just living up to his [her brother's] expectations and my family's expectations."

This latter source of worth also influenced how she conceptualized her purpose. She said that two of her purposes in life were to "make myself proud [and] make my family proud." Yet she admitted regarding these purposes, "Finding how to do that is what I'm still looking for." When we asked her if she had any idea of what that might look like, Susan noted, "Well, I'm already enrolled in pre-med here, so that, I think, made both myself proud and my family proud." Her answer made me wonder if she would feel the freedom to change her major if she realized she no longer wanted to pursue pre-med.

Her focus on pleasing her parents and family may stem from the fact that her parents divorced when she was in high school. She shared, "My brother was having a really hard time with it. So, I think being there for him was another thing that helped me want to be a role model for him." This event also influenced her vision of the good life in the future. Ten years from now, she wanted "to have my own house somewhere. Not really sure where that is yet . . . I would still either be in medical school or just getting out, so finding, you know, a good job from that. And just, you know, have a couple of dogs, living with my friends, going out, being mentally happy." She did not see herself moving into marriage or having children in the next decade.

Later in the interview, she noted that she was involved in her church's youth groups. As a result, she volunteered a bit. Throughout the interview, however, she never mentioned how Christianity influenced or played a role in how she thinks about her worth, purpose, or vision of the good life. If there was an adult who spoke into her life, it was her grandmother. She shared, "We live with her, so she's been there all my life. And I think she is just good at looking at things from both sides. . . . She's not afraid to tell me that I'm in the wrong. But she's also there to be, like, 'Okay, you are probably wrong for doing that, but here's either how to fix it, or what to do next time.' So, I think she calls me on my BS." In this regard, she found not only worth and purpose in her family but also her major source of accountability.

Most young emerging adults try to find themselves in one of two ways. They attempt to self-author their lives, or they strive to socially author their lives. What do I mean? They either try to figure out their source of worth, their purpose, and their vision of the good life themselves, or they rely on other people to inform these things.

Erin's story from the introduction provides an example of a student trying to self-author her life. She derived her worth from her accomplishments, and her purpose related to accomplishing more things. In Susan's story, from the beginning of this chapter, we see the other approach. She looks to other people for her worth and purpose, although she appears to have chosen her vision of the good life primarily on her own. She does have her grandmother to thank for mentorship and advice, but her grandmother's guidance seems centered on avoiding unwise choices rather than developing a positive vision of her flourishing. Although you could argue that finding worth in your family is better than other sources, such as social media or wayward peers, the problem with self-authored and socially authored approaches to life is that these sources prove unstable. Relying on others means that changing relationships can shift your sense of worth or purpose—in both Erin's and Susan's stories, their families experienced tragic fracturing.

As a result, both self-authored and socially authored approaches fail to provide vital fundamentals that you will need throughout your life: a stable foundation for worth (for both you and others), guidance about how to find your purpose and vocation, and a clear motivation for and understanding of what goods to pursue in life and why. This chapter draws on my and others' research to illustrate these pitfalls among contemporary college students in the first area: your source of worth and value.

What Is Your Source of Worth and Value?

When emerging adults enter college, hardly any of them doubt their worth and value. My research team has asked hundreds of college students across the nation this question: *From where do you derive your worth and value?* We have had only one student who admitted, "I don't know, I feel like for a long time I sometimes struggle with that or kind of slip into a kind of nihilistic spiral—nothing matters, I don't matter."

Every other person has answered that they derive their worth and value from particular sources.

Most answers, even for Christian students, fall into two problematic approaches: deriving value and worth from identities based on social relationships (social authorship) and from the identities a person has determined for themself (self-authorship). The reason these sources are problematic is that they are unstable and contingent on others' views of you or your performance.

Social Authorship

Ashley was a twenty-two-year-old senior at a private Christian university when we talked to her. She identified as a Christian, but what really seemed to interest her pertained to Greek life on campus. Not having anyone in her family who had pledged before, she had asked others for advice: "I was told by everyone to go into it with an open mind and, you know, let the process decide or whatever, which is a lot of BS. You have to be strategic. You have to have connections. And you have to work really hard to get into a sorority that is what you want or that is acceptable to you." Since she was not initially strategic, she rushed. "I got the bottom sorority. . . . A lot of the girls were stereotypically unattractive, happened to be overweight, or didn't have much wealth, or a combination of those things." She said, "I really put an effort to try to connect with these people. And it really wasn't working. And also, I didn't like the idea of being seen on campus as someone who was the last pick. That made me uncomfortable and kind of sad. So, I ended up dropping that sorority."

The next time she rushed, she related, "I'm strategic. I go to the pre-rush events. I meet girls in the sorority I want to get into, and I do get the sorority that I want. And the day comes, it's awesome. I really feel like I've found a lot of friends and that I can grow my bonds with them over time. And I feel like I'm belonging. I decided to sign a lease with some girls from my sorority." In short, she achieves what she believes is her social dream and is accepted by the group to which she wants to be accepted.

Sadly, Ashley soon realized she did not fit in with this sorority either: "I'm living with these girls, and it becomes apparent to me very quickly over time that they are much wealthier than I have ever even imagined. And they are unaware of it. They threw out my stuff in the refrigerator because they thought it was bad. And then I was like, 'I can't afford to replace this. And also why would you throw out a bottle of ketchup? It's ketchup, it doesn't expire after a month.'" The difficulties went beyond food:

> They would spend money on the stupidest things. Like one time, they spent $80 each on a 30-day juice cleanse that they didn't even finish, and that filled up our entire refrigerator with bad juice. They would constantly be getting packages in from Urban Outfitters. . . . But for someone like me, that's not somewhere I can even think of shopping. When we thrifted together, they would mostly just make fun of the clothes in the thrift store. They wouldn't actually shop. And when I wanted to try stuff on, they would act as if those clothes were dirty. And it was like gross for me to try them on.
>
> They all drove new cars, one of which she got into an accident and her car was totaled, and she had a new car within the next week. They were selfish and entitled, and really, really mean to me, so mean that I ended up getting into a pretty bad depressive spiral. . . . I found out later on that they had a group chat without me, where they would just say mean things about me. The girl that I shared a room with is now dating my ex-boyfriend. And she would have him over without telling me and I would get home from work—which none of them have jobs—I would get home from work, and he would be there in my room. And I looked like I just came home from work. They were all really callous and horrible. And it hurt twice as much because these girls had rushed me for this sorority. And they had told me that we're sisters and stuff like that. And they entirely betrayed my trust.

Ashley had worked so hard to belong to a social group, but the group ended up betraying her. The consequences led her to spiral into mental health problems.

Social authorship is quite understandable. Most of how you understand yourself has been defined by others. Your parents named you. You inherit family histories, religion, state and national histories, and identity group histories (e.g., Christian, American, Texan, African American, female). You cannot simply discard these inherited aspects of your identity, nor should you. Indeed, there are good aspects of all those identities and their associated histories.

In addition, the various social groups you encounter are also in the business of defining who you are. Of course, they are not overt about it, but the environment they create encourages you at the same time to be a social author. By *social author*, I mean these social contexts require you to make important choices about your identity, and because of those choices, you make other commitments about what it means to be excellent in that identity. Such a commitment involves following certain rules, acquiring certain virtues or avoiding particular vices, and engaging in deliberate practices that help you achieve excellence.

To provide an example, once you are labeled a college student, you are asked to follow the college's rules; uphold the virtue of academic honesty necessary to be a student; acquire or practice virtues such as intellectual humility, perseverance, self-control, or wisdom; and engage in certain practices such as studying, group work, and writing papers. Similarly, the college will give you a menu of majors, and once you decide to choose one (or more), it is the university's responsibility to help you start on the road to becoming excellent in that professional identity (e.g., an excellent biologist, accountant, sociologist). Moreover, universities will teach you the basic professional ethics code of an academic discipline. You do not simply determine for yourself what it means to be a good biologist, accountant, or social worker (or else you would not need to attend a university).

But universities do more than define you in these basic ways. They may alter their treatment of you based on an entire range of other identities, such as your state, national, racial, sexual, or religious identity. This treatment may come from administrative decisions, the academic curriculum, student life offices (e.g., first-gen college student), or fellow students. For example, you can choose from various student groups, but each one of these will tell you what it means to be in a particular fraternity, sorority, athletic club, service group, academic honor society, or whatever organization you choose to join. Certain friend groups also invite you to engage in particular practices. All these different identities will already have existing traditions telling you what it means to flourish in a particular identity. These messages can be, and often are, implicit.

Thus, in college, you will be faced with a tournament of selves—all calling you to be a certain kind of person. These groups, organizations, or institutions will inform you about what it means to be an excellent student, professional, American, friend, neighbor, racial/ethnic group member, woman or man, steward of your finances, or caretaker of the earth, to name a few examples. Even if you have rejected your prior identities and sources of wisdom after interrogating them with your newfound knowledge, your identity will still be influenced by some of these already existing collegiate visions.

Now, it is one thing to recognize these social influences and submit to them in portions of your life, but it is another thing to allow them to define all of who you are and who you should be. The students who socially author their lives are the ones who allow these various groups to define their fundamental value and worth. In other words, they obtain their worth through these relationships and what people say about them. When my team and I identified these students in our research, we noticed they fell into four groups that derived their worth from others in different ways.

The first group obtains their worth through family relationships such as parents, siblings, or one's family in general. Below are some example quotes from some of these respondents.

- Parents: "Having conversations with my parents . . . for right now that's like been one of few little things that have made me feel what I think is worthwhile."
- Siblings: "But I feel like getting a small bit of validation from just one of my little siblings, it means more to me than a lot of things. Probably means more than it should."
- Family in general: "My family very much. Because I think that they value me."

Although students have little to no control over these forms of familial relationships, they use them to derive their worth and value.

A second group finds their identity and worth through their relationships with friends or a particular social group (such as Ashley). One student summarized her source of worth and value as "words of affirmation from my friends." Another student noted, "I'd say I think the people I surround myself with, so probably my friends. . . . I think that surrounding myself with people who are positive and encouraging and just generally uplifting. Those types of people make me feel valued and loved." The key is that other people are the ones who make them feel noticed and worthwhile. One African American student shared that she feels worthwhile and valuable when "someone that sees me and sees my race as an opportunity and not as a burden. Makes me feel seen. . . . I think people that like genuinely want to know about my life and that care about my well-being." The obvious danger with deriving worth in this way is that relationships may fail to provide love, value, or notice at times and thus fail to supply a sense of worth.

The third group derives worth from how people in general respond to their actions. This approach can involve what one student called being the "life of the party": "The thing that makes me feel worthwhile and valuable is the energy and the joy that I like to bring to a room. . . . I enjoy, I don't know, bringing a positive energy when I go places, and I feel that I do that and, yeah, what makes me feel worthwhile is bringing a positive energy when I can." But there are problems here too: What happens when the people at the party do not respond the way you hoped? Or worse, what happens when there is no party?

For the fourth group, their relational accomplishments had less to do with entertaining people and more to do with helping others. For instance, one student shared, "I feel the most valuable when I am helping others through life. I am really driven by other people. When helping others, or kind of even just giving them the shoulder to cry on or someone to listen." Another student told us, "So, I think my value to me at least personally depends a lot on what I can do for other people." Of course, helping others is a wonderful thing. The problem is placing one's worth in these activities. If a person ever fails at these relational accomplishments, their sense of value may plummet as well.

In this respect, there is often an odd, codependent relationship established with the helper. These people always need to feel needed (e.g., "feeling like I'm needed from my boyfriend or my siblings or my mom"). One student named Jessica shared with us, "I like others to need me. I like doing things for other people. I don't know. Something small, like 'Oh, I need you to bring me a snack before my class.' I'll go, 'I'll get you a snack. I'll run and bring it to you.' But then also just like emotionally too. I want people to want to come and talk to me about things. So, I like feeling needed in that way and in that capacity as well." The challenge Jessica and other helpers face is how to find their worth when they no longer feel needed.

In reality, all four approaches face one core challenge: They depend on others who may change their views about you or your actions. All four depend on what scholars call *contingent* sources of self-worth—meaning they depend on your circumstances at any given moment. Thus, your worth could go up or down based on how others are thinking of you now or whether they affirm or need you.

Self-Authorship

The self-authors are different. They find their worth in accomplishments or contributing to the world through their gifts and abilities. They derive value from things such as "being intelligent," "achieving academically," "how good I am in sports," "building stuff with my hands," or "my accomplishments." One college senior succinctly summarized this view: "I feel worthwhile and valuable when I am able to succeed at the things that I try to do."

Often, these achievements are good things. For instance, a few students find their worth and value in "just making change, however small, change for the better." Some students even have this view concerning their relationship with God: "Like when I read the Bible and when I am praying, I feel very loved and valued by God." This student equated God's love and value with practicing certain Christian disciplines. Similarly, a Muslim student shared with us, "As Muslims, we have to pray five times a day. So, I do that. I also read the Qur'an, which is our holy book. And I try to make sure that I'm living my life fulfilling the guidelines that are implemented through the Qur'an." Any kind of religious believer can turn to achievement to find worth and value.

Of course, the reality that these "self-authors" do not always acknowledge is that the standards of achievement or success they are trying to fulfill are still set by external social groups, other people, or even their interpretation of their religious deity's or deities' requirements. In fact, this approach is intelligible only within a particular type of culture that sets up standards for success. You do not create the standards for athletic, musical, or professional excellence on your own. Others have already established them.

Oddly, education scholars promote the idea that a successful student has made their own identity choices and is thereby "self-authored."[1] Ironically, there is even a whole academic theory that promotes the concept of self-authorship as being what a person should hope to undergo and achieve in college.[2]

Granted, one of the reasons for this emphasis is that although students in K–12 education have slowly been learning how to be independent, they still rely heavily on their parents and communities of origin for guidance. This is certainly true in the moral realm. When we ask students in their first month of college about their sources of moral knowledge and wisdom, we find that they refer to the social sources one would expect—parents ("I know I can always turn to my mom. She's always available. I can just hit her name in my phone and call her and say, 'Hey. I'm struggling with this. Can you give me some advice?'"), siblings (e.g., "My older brother, since he's been through it. He's been through all my problems pretty much because we relate so much."), teachers or other trusted adults from their community (e.g., "I used a lot of my high school teachers as sounding boards."), and trusted friends (e.g., "My close friends and probably some longer-lasting friendships from back home because they know me better right now than my new friends.").

Yet certain developmental scholars claim that as adolescents move into emerging adulthood, they need to abandon the older sources that socially authored them in order to find themselves. In this view, one must learn to think critically and make decisions on one's own to a greater extent than before. Indeed, a well-known higher education theorist, Vincent Tinto, claimed, "In order to become fully incorporated in the life of the college, individuals have to physically as well as socially dissociate themselves from the communities of the past."[3] This dissociation, he believed, involved a person's previous identities and communities, since "such communities differ from college not only in composition but also

1. Marcia B. Baxter Magolda, *Making Their Own Way: Narratives for Transforming Higher Education to Promote Self-Development* (Stylus, 2001).

2. Baxter Magolda, *Making Their Own Way.*

3. Vincent Tinto, *Leaving College: Rethinking the Causes and Cures of Student Attrition*, 2nd ed. (University of Chicago Press, 1993), 96.

in the values, norms, and behavioral and intellectual styles that characterize their everyday life. As a result, the process leading to the adoption of behaviors and norms appropriate to the life of the college necessarily requires some degree of transformation and perhaps a rejection of the norms of past communities."[4] There is some truth to this point. After all, we need to learn to think critically about our past—what was good, fallen, and/or redemptive.

The problem comes when someone derives their worth and value from being a self-author.

When you fail or are not able to contribute, what happens to your sense of worth? We know the answer to this question from empirical studies. In a sample of elite athletes, researchers found that those with performance-based self-narrative profiles (i.e., self-worth dependent on performance) had the highest levels of depression, anxiety, and shame as well as the lowest life satisfaction.[5] People will not always be successful, so the self-author's sense of worth and value always fluctuates.

The Problems with Contingent Worth

Scholars call all these sources of worth, both self-authored and socially authored sources, *external* or *contingent*. Your worth goes up and down based on what others think or say, or what your grades or recent achievements are. Not surprisingly, scholars have also discovered that students who derive their worth from these contingent or external sources are more likely to experience mental health problems such as anxiety and depression.[6] These students perform to please others or to make themselves feel worthwhile,

4. Tinto, *Leaving College*, 96.

5. Benjamin J. Houltberg, Kenneth T. Wang, Wei Qi, and Christina S. Nelson, "Self-Narrative Profiles of Elite Athletes and Comparisons on Psychological Well-Being," *Research Quarterly for Exercise and Sport* 89, no. 3 (2018): 354–60.

6. Sarah K. Dixon and Sharon E. Robinson Kurpius, "Depression and College Stress Among University Undergraduates: Do Mattering and Self-Esteem Make a Difference?," *Journal of College Student Development* 49, no. 5 (2008): 412–24, https://doi.org/10.1353/csd.0.0024; Prathma Sharma, Kirin Uzar, and Gina M. Brelsford, "Self-Esteem, Grit, and Optimism: Predictors of Depression and Anxiety in Emerging Adults," *Journal of College Student Development* 62, no. 5 (2021): 563–74, https://doi.org/10.1353/csd.2021.0053.

or they believe they must constantly strive to maintain their worth and value. Research has found that depression and suicide risk are higher for students with these more contingent and less secure sources of worth.[7]

Moreover, the worth and value they must try to maintain usually come at the expense of other people and groups. Someone's accomplishments, social tribe (e.g., family, nationality, race/ethnicity, gender, social class, political orientation, profession), or relational accomplishments distinguish one as different from others. Unfortunately, this kind of worth creation tends to ostracize and dehumanize those without these accomplishments, those outside one's social tribe, or those who cannot achieve certain relational accomplishments. Neither individual nor social construction of our worth provides us with a defense against our tendency to dehumanize other people.

If your worth depends on the approval of others, what happens when a group considers you the problem race, sex, or tribe and simply wants to discount your worth and value? I mentioned the student who shared that she feels worth and value when "someone . . . sees me and sees my race as an opportunity and not as a burden." However, what happens when that does not occur? The person who has socially constructed their worth has no solid foundation.

Now, I should confess that I, too, faced this problem in college. I ended my senior year of high school as a valedictorian, a basketball and baseball player, and someone with numerous friends. I ended my first semester of college as an occasional intramural player and a B- student in an engineering major I later left, and I had a few new friends in a place where I initially did not know anyone. It became clear to me that I could not hang my worth on my accomplishments or relationships.

Who can save us from the contingencies of social and self-authorship and give us a stable source of worth? Before going straight to answering that, I want to spend some time in the next chapter discussing two other major problems with these sources of worth. These problems involve how self-authorship and social authorship relate to one's purpose and one's conception of the good life.

7. Chad E. Lakey, Jameson K. Hirsch, Lyndsay A. Nelson, and Sheri A. Nsamenang, "Effects of Contingent Self-Esteem on Depressive Symptoms and Suicidal Behavior," *Death Studies* 38, no. 9 (2014): 563–70.

CHAPTER TWO

The Second Problem with Losing Yourself

Missing or Disordered Purposes

> I have a sense of purpose, but I'm not really sure what the purpose is, to be honest.
>
> —Maria, American college student

What is your purpose? I spend part of my research time asking college students that question. I find it a particularly important question, especially because one of the current problems facing emerging adults today concerns their sense of purpose. *The Wall Street Journal* recently reported that over 30 percent of US twelfth graders now "wonder if there is a purpose to life given [the] world situation." That is the highest number recorded in the past half century.[1]

Entering college does not always help these students find their purpose. Studies find that anywhere from 20 to 25 percent of college students

1. Andrew Restuccia and Eliza Collins, "The Rough Years That Turned Gen Z into America's Most Disillusioned Voters," *Wall Street Journal*, March 15, 2024, https://www.wsj.com/politics/elections/gen-z-voters-election-tiktok-5bcdc524. The data comes from Jean M. Twenge, *Generations: The Real Differences Between Gen Z, Millennials, Gen X, Boomers, and Silents—and What They Mean for America's Future* (Simon & Schuster, 2023).

do not know their purpose.[2] I find the purposeless especially among the nonreligious students I interview. They confess things such as

- "I think that the whole purpose thing is foggy in my head right now."
- "I am still trying to figure it out. I feel like I need to acquire a purpose, obviously to feel fulfilled, but I don't really know what that purpose is yet."
- "I'm not fully decided or set on what my purpose is, I guess."

Of course, there are also religious students who answer this way as well.

Among those who do indicate a purpose, many choose to draw their purpose from several dominant cultural scripts. These cobbled-together understandings, however, fail to provide not only a sense of worth but also clear ways of thinking about their purpose. As a result, this approach still leaves them searching for motivation and purpose through their accomplishments and relationships, without a clear understanding of who they are and who they should become. The reason for this struggle emerged in our interviews with these students. Like worth, we find two major groups divided into self-authored, self-focused purpose choosers and socially focused purpose selectors.

Self-Authored and Self-Focused

Self-authors want to create their purpose from scratch. As Gabby shared with us, "I think I create my own life's purpose. I don't know if mine in particular has a greater meaning in the universe, but I think that by doing things that I find value [in], I create purpose." Their purpose is not something that others provide for them, including God. Kelly admitted to me in an interview, "I don't have a purpose in my life, because I don't have any religion, but I do feel like I live for myself."

Like Kelly, if self-authors do have a purpose, the ends they pursue are then related to self-focused outcomes such as personal career goals,

2. Perry L. Glanzer, Jonathan P. Hill, and Byron R. Johnson, *The Quest for Purpose: The Collegiate Search for a Meaningful Life* (State University of New York Press, 2017), 159.

money, comfort, security, pleasure, or happiness. For John, he wanted to do things that would lead to happiness and wealth: "I would like to do things. Graduate, get a job. If I'm not happy with that job, I will eventually move on to a better-paying or more rewarding and fulfilling job. Build a retirement fund, but not actually retire. Just have money in an account, because I think that retired people die before those who don't retire." For Ken, those material things were a sign of achievement in life. He said for his purpose he wanted "a good job, nice cars, [and a] nice house. Just really being accomplished . . . Having those things would make me happy."

Aisha shared that what drove her was a different set of self-focused goals. "I always live by what I have to do immediately. I always make a lot of lists, like things I have to get done. So, I have a short-term list and more of a long-term list. By this time, I have to apply to these places or do these job interviews. . . . So you're trying to create a type of stability by having a job already laid out for you once you graduate. So it's all about your comforts." At the end of her self-authored list appeared to be stability and comfort.

For others, this self-oriented focus simply involved chasing their feelings, as illustrated by a student whose purpose involved "following things that I'm passionate about and not focusing so much on applications and grad school and jobs and money and stuff like that, but really just doing what will make me happy." For others, like Angie, it means, "I know that I want to get a good job, I want to be successful." In all these cases, however, the focus of their pursuit is on themselves. Not surprisingly, studies reveal eighteen- to twenty-three-year-olds are increasingly narcissistic, disconnected from and unaware of moral traditions of thought, and lacking in purpose.[3]

That's not the only mental problem. When self-focused students fail at their purpose, mental health issues can follow. Tom shared how this happened to him: "I actually was recruited by [my university] to wrestle originally and spent my whole life in that sport. I was pretty good at it. I did really good in high school and was nationally ranked and everything.

3. Christian Smith with Kari M. Hojara, Hilary A. Davidson, and Patricia Snell Herzog, *Lost in Transition: The Dark Side of Emerging Adulthood* (Oxford University Press, 2011); Glanzer, Hill, and Johnson, *Quest for Purpose*.

I got recruited by [my university] and when I got here, I have to say, I came in pre-med, and I was trying to do as much of everything as possible because I think my motivation and my purpose in life was like: If I couldn't maximize my potential in every domain simultaneously then life wasn't really worth it. I definitely dealt with much more depression back then."

This outlook then extends to later in life. Hollister provides an example of this process. Although an older master's student at the time of our interview, he admitted regarding his life purpose, "It's definitely something I'm still trying to figure out." He had tried self-oriented purposes: "For a great amount of time, it was tied to work and school. But after a while, you feel like this is not very fulfilling, as much as you think it would be." He went on to share,

> So, yeah. I would say I was always an A student; I was very career-oriented and degree-oriented, and work-oriented. But throughout the years, after graduating from undergrad and working, I worked for like four or five years before doing my master's, it changed. I realized the general thought is that you get a good job, you make a lot of money, and then you'll be happy. So, I realized that that's not true at all. You can have a good job, good pay, and everything, and you always have this feeling that you'll get there, and this is where you'll finally be okay. I'm good, I don't need to work more, but that's not true. You always have something that you're working towards.

He had still not found the ultimate end to which he was working.

Unfortunately, we found in a Gallup national survey of college students that we commissioned, self-oriented purposes filled more than half of the top eight purposes, including the number one spot (see table 2.1).

TABLE 2.1

Top Self-Oriented Purposes of US College Students (n = 2,503)

The purpose of my life is to	Strongly Agree
1. be happy	81
3. experience life to the fullest	67
6. achieve success in my career	55
7. maintain a comfortable standard of living	48
8. discover new things about the world	47

Source: Perry L. Glanzer, Jonathan P. Hill, and Byron R. Johnson, *The Quest for Purpose: The Collegiate Search for a Meaningful Life* (State University of New York Press, 2017), 147.

I do not mean to say that all of these things are necessarily bad. As a father, I too want my sons to achieve success in their careers and discover new things about the world. But making self-oriented goals the central focus of one's purpose leads to a selfish, unfaithful, and unfulfilling life.

Socially Focused Purposes

The socially focused student derives their purpose from others, such as friends (e.g., "My purpose is to develop relationships because relationships are what make life worth living.") and family (e.g., "Have a family, kids, grandkids."), or from service to others (e.g., "I always felt like my purpose was to help people."). Christie provides an example of someone who combined all three. When asked about her life purpose, she shared, "I would have to say personal relationships with people are kind of what keeps me going, kind of my purpose for living. I love personal relationships with people, acquaintances you just see sometimes, people with whom you have deep conversations a lot of times. I'm close to my parents, so my family members. I'd say that's probably it, and especially if you're like volunteering."

Other students, such as Ava and Mark, focused on one set of relationships. Ava told us, "I think I'm very big in succeeding in my career because my parents, my whole family are immigrants, and I think that my purpose is to kind of make the immigration worth it or make something out of it." Similarly, Mark shared, "But my main purpose . . . I really focus on the closest people in my life—so the closest people in my life are probably my family. And so, I really want to help them in any way I possibly can, whether that's financially or just helping them reach their full potential."

Occasionally, these students would see moving from self-oriented purposes to socially oriented purposes as a better developmental step. Soren shared this developmental journey:

> I think that pre-college or kind of leading into college, early college, I think I was developing or getting purpose from the idea of being influential. I feel like we're kind of primed that way with higher education. Make your mark on the world. Change the world. And just kind of,

> I'm going to have all of these cool ideas and impress people and have important things to say. Or like I was playing in a band, and I mean we just played at coffee shops and stuff, but I think I had hubris about wanting to make it and be interviewed and be famous or something. All the American Dream, but it was kind of a weird niche intellectual arts space. Even if I wouldn't have admitted it to myself then, I think I wanted that.
>
> Whereas now . . . I care more about the people directly in front of me than some external validation. I guess I find a lot of meaning in relationships that go beyond just trivial kind of niceties. Like, meaningful connection with other human beings, specifically, I mean family. . . . At times when I've been struggling in that area, grounding myself in love and care for people close to me, even if I might not see that in my own self, is helpful. So, my nephew or siblings, or parents.

As I will discuss in chapter 10, these other-oriented purposes are better for one's flourishing.[4] But when they serve as a source of worth, they are insufficient.

Finding one's purpose in relationships is also not quite as pervasive as self-oriented purposes. Still, in our nationally representative Gallup-commissioned poll, we found that caring for the family, helping others, and building lasting relationships were three of the top five purposes among college students (see table 2.2).

4. For a review of this literature, please consult Anthony L. Burrow and Patrick L. Hill, "Purpose as a Form of Identity Capital for Positive Youth Adjustment," *Developmental Psychology* 47, no. 4 (2011): 1196; Lisa Kiang, "Deriving Daily Purpose Through Daily Events and Role Fulfillment Among Asian American Youth," *Journal of Research on Adolescence* 22, no. 1 (2012): 185–98; Kendall Cotton Bronk, Patrick L. Hill, Daniel K. Lapsley, Tasneem L. Talib, and Holmes Finch, "Purpose, Hope, and Life Satisfaction in Three Age Groups," *The Journal of Positive Psychology* 4, no. 6 (2009): 500–510; Anthony L. Burrow, Amanda C. O'Dell, and Patrick L. Hill, "Profiles of a Developmental Asset: Youth Purpose as a Context for Hope and Well-Being," *Journal of Youth and Adolescence* 39, no. 11 (2010): 1265–73; Kendall Cotton Bronk, "The Role of Purpose in Life in Healthy Identity Formation: A Grounded Model," *New Directions for Youth Development* 2011, no. 132 (2011): 31–44; Ann S. Masten, and Marie-Gabrielle Reed, "Resilience in Development," *Handbook of Positive Psychology* (2002): 74–88.

TABLE 2.2

Top Relational Purposes of US College Students (n = 2,503)

The purpose of my life is to	Strongly Agree
2. care for a family	70
4. help others	58
5. build lasting friendships	57

Source: Perry L. Glanzer, Jonathan P. Hill, and Byron R. Johnson, *The Quest for Purpose: The Collegiate Search for a Meaningful Life* (State University of New York Press, 2017), 147.

Again, I want to be clear. These purposes are all healthy aspects of a flourishing life. Moreover, even better than self-focused purposes, these purposes are correlated with a flourishing life. The danger of this approach, though, is that your purpose hinges on the responses of other people. For example, Jose noted that his purpose was "making my friends happy. . . . In my brother's graduating class, the valedictorian, I barely remember his speech. I barely remember anything, but this has stuck with me. If you can't be happy yourself, the best thing to do is make other people happy. . . . So, I try to make my friends as happy as possible." The problem that Jose will face is that whether he fulfills his purpose depends on the happiness of his friends—something that can constantly change. We should still pursue relationships, careers, and service, but those are sub-purposes that distract or constrain visions of a more ultimate source of purpose and worth.

Determining the Good Life

Finally, there is also a problem shared by both the self- and other-focused students, beyond issues of self-worth and purpose. It involves how they determine the good life. By "good life," I mean an overall vision of what flourishing would be like in the present and the future. Some people think of "good" as involving a moral quality in their life, but others think of "good" as simply involving material comforts, relational achievements, or pleasures. In our research, we have found that the individually and socially authored and focused students we interviewed perceived the good life as having little to do with the moral dimensions of life. Instead, it had to do with either ambiguous personal goals for self-authors, such as what I label the "Happy Strivers" or "Comfort Strivers," or cultural scripts such as "the American Dream" for social authors.[5]

Self-Authorship and the Good Life

Self-authored students envision the good life as a set of personal goals to reach. Much like a set of ingredients in a recipe, they believe that if they mix these individual ingredients with a few from the social ingredients (e.g., marriage), they will find a good life. These self-authored ingredients include

1. Having a career, sometimes additionally characterized by one of these two qualities:
    a. Passionate about (e.g., "Hopefully I'm in love with my job.")
    b. Stable (e.g., "I just want a stable career.")
2. Being financially stable or independent (e.g., "Financially stable would definitely be the good life.")
3. Being wealthy (e.g., "Okay, this is going to be a very materialistic answer. Being successful to me is like having a good salary. Got to be able to take care of yourself.")
4. Living in a certain geographic place (e.g., "Hopefully be back in New York City—I love that city a lot.")
5. Being fit or healthy (e.g., "To be fit, because I love exercising. When I see a mother and she's fit, I'm just like, 'Wow, I really want to be like that' . . . You know, like Wonder Woman.")
6. Traveling (e.g., "Going on vacation, every now and then. . . . I want to see more of the world.")
7. Achieving a certain level of general stability or comfort (e.g., "Ten years from now, the biggest word that I can think of is stability. I want to make sure that my life won't fall apart.")

5. Some of the quotes and the analysis that is the basis for these conclusions can be found in Perry L. Glanzer, Theodore F. Cockle, Sarah Schnitker, and Jonathan Hill, "American College Students' Understandings of the Good Life: A Grounded Theory," *Journal of Beliefs and Values* 45, no. 4 (2024): 636–56, https://doi:10.1080/13617672.2023.2212358.

8. Learning (e.g., "I feel like learning is always going to be part of my life; if I'm not learning, I kind of feel like stuck, you know, knowledge is big to me.")
9. Enjoying hobbies (e.g., "Having enough free time to do things that I'd enjoy like hobbies," and "I'd like to live near the University of Maine and go to all the hockey games.")
10. Being happy (e.g., "For me, I think my main goal, or my main idea of like, a successful life is for me, at the end of every day to be able to say that I am happy.")

This last ingredient is particularly important for a group I call the *Happy Strivers*. Although they picked anywhere from one to eight ingredients, they were all subsumed under the main ingredient of happiness (e.g., "I'm happy. I guess that's the big thing.").

What makes them different is that they qualify or sum up all those ingredients by noting that they were evaluating them based on whether those ingredients would make them happy: "I really hope that I've graduated from law school, and that I'm working for a successful firm. I don't necessarily want to say that I want to be married or have kids yet, but I would hope that my life is stable, so I want to have my own place to live. I want to know that I have a steady income, I'm not worried about putting food on the table, and *overall that I'd be genuinely happy*, whether that means that I just have friends or that I'm married" (emphasis added).

The ingredients could also be quite varied and include traveling and eating healthy food and being fit. Adrianna, a senior envisioning the good life ten years out, provided this example:

> I get to set my own hours, or I will just go to work, and I will not want to leave work once I get there. I think being able to pay my own bills. That'd be fun. To set trips and actually go on them. . . . I know that I would like to travel; being able to travel and not have to worry about like I planned a trip, and I can't even go on it. I don't know. Eating good food. *Just being genuinely happy with the situation that I'm in*, or at least being content with where I am right now in life. *So, in the next ten years, I just want to be happy with where I am and happy with what I've done so far to get where I am that day.* (emphasis added)

The interesting thing about Happy Strivers, as evidenced by Adrianna's "I don't know," is that they are not always sure what will lead them to find happiness.

The positive emotions associated with happiness are what they were after, especially in contrast with the negative emotions that come with certain parts of life. Julie contrasted her desire to be happy with being stressed: "I would be . . . happy in terms of I would be less stressed. My constant state of being would not be a stressed state of being. Sometimes it feels like I'm stressed all the time now and I would think in five years, if I was living the good life, I would be slightly less stressed." Another student did not offer any ingredients other than happiness and simply went to the bottom line: "I don't have any specifics, and I think I'd hate myself if I did because odds are I'm not going to have that, but in general like I just want to be in a place where I am happy."

Closely related to but distinct from Happiness Strivers are *Comfort and Stability Seekers*. Like Julie, these students also want to be free of stress, but they articulate their overall meta-ingredient in terms of comfort and/or stability. Interestingly, I found students who spoke about the theme of comfort and stability often focused on these elements because they had grown up without them. They looked for ingredient combinations, such as a stable career and family, that would be a source of stability and comfort. Andres, a microbiology student at a public university, shared his five-year desire.

> I would say, having a family, hopefully fiancé, wife, maybe kids. I'd say having a decent home, like growing up I know how it is to struggle, so I just want to live in like a decent house. I don't want like a mansion, or like two houses. I don't want things like that. I just want something that I can live comfortably in. A nice car, maybe, not an extravagant car, just a nice car. I just want to be able to live comfortably without having to live paycheck to paycheck like my mother did. That would be the good life for me in five years.

A senior named Jason said something similar: "And the other thing would be to be financially stable. I grew up in a low-income household, and I don't ever want for my kids for money to be a barrier to what they want to do. So, just to be in a place where I am comfortable but also have a little wiggle room for some extra things aside of that. So those are the two main things, I would say."

It was not always past experiences that made students resort to this view of the good life. Sometimes it was the future. Matt, a senior sharing his ten-year vision, looked less to his difficult financial past but more to his uncertain financial future: "So, I think a good life that's flourishing would be in a financially stable position. Not because making money is important, but just because going to [this university] for the last four years, that's a . . . fair amount of loans, and just understand that that's something I have to, pretty soon here, start dealing with. Hopefully, ten years from now, I'm just at a spot where it's not something that's causing myself and maybe my future family any type of stress or anxiety." Overall, this group was less focused on positive dreams and more focused on avoiding the negative realities of their past in their future.

In some cases, these Comfort and Stability Seekers go as far as to oppose adding certain social ingredients that might impinge on this comfort, such as children. Angie, a student at a public university who is majoring in engineering, shared the characteristic good life dream of these students: "Well, first things first, (1) I'd like to have a job I enjoy doing. (2) still be single, . . . marriage is forever, and that's a pretty big deal to them, unlike some people who kind of go through their lives, that's kind of mean, so a job that I enjoy, be single; (3) make enough money to be living comfortably, like I don't need to be making like $100,000 or anything, but I don't want to be like I'm struggling to have to pay rent in not a very nice place, just like always having to worry about that."

Similarly, Jenny wanted to limit her family obligations to maintain her comfort: "I would like to have a house and be comfortable in my house and not worry about how to pay for it. Um, I would like to have a job that I'm happy in. I would have at least three dogs cause crucial. I don't know about kids, cause that's just horrifying. I'll stick to the dogs and like the boyfriend's cat, but we'll stick with that." Another student, Andrew, shared, "It's pretty simple. I think having kind of your temporal needs met first is pretty important. Having a stable income that covers you day-to-day and times of need, and maybe just a little bit extra for entertainment and that sort of thing. Probably living with a significant other. . . . A job that is challenging has a bit of creativity in it and will afford me time off. No kids." These students all want to self-author their good life by reducing it to combining self-authored ingredients.

Social Authorship and the Good Life

Socially authored students rely on relational scripts supplied by various cultural narratives to determine their understanding of the good life. These scripts also usually involve adding goals to their list of good life ingredients, such as marriage and children (e.g., "I would be happy knowing that I raised a family."), friendships (i.e., "Having a good social life."), and often owning pets (e.g., "At least three dogs.").

The most popular script combines the following ingredients: career success, marriage, kids, friends, some degree of material success, and/or living in a certain location. I call these students the *American Dreamers* because many of them specifically described their vision of the good life as the "American Dream." Here is one such statement from Margaret, who described the good life ten years out: "I'd be married. Absolutely have a kid or two at that point, so not five. I probably won't have like four or five kids. But yeah, you know, I mean, like the American Dream. A person people look up to, a person that people respect . . . be pursuing a lucrative career both financially and personally."

Henry described his vision: "I guess kind of like the American Dream is kind of the idea, you know, family, kids, big house, car, nice cars, vacation every summer, uh, stuff like that. But to me, a good family, good life, for me personally, it would just be having someone in a relationship that I can really pour my love into. And being able to be like financially stable and not have to worry about that kind of thing." Of course, others described their vision of the American Dream without labeling it and just provided similar types of ingredients.

The difficulty, of course, with reaching this socially authored vision of the good life is that other people do not always cooperate. You may not marry, have children, or enjoy the friendships you want. Even pets get sick and die, and they can be unaffordable or impractical at certain stages of life. Thus, you may find yourself chasing a vision that cannot be fully achieved.

Overall, both the self-authored and socially authored approaches to finding purpose in one's life have problems. The problem with this self-authored approach is that the autonomous, self-authored life proves unfulfilling and even mentally unstable. We find our greatest meaning, purpose, and flourishing through social commitments and communities. Human flourishing is foundationally rooted in others and social involvement, and as a result, self-authorship proves insufficient for deriving our worth, purpose, and view of the good life.

The socially authored approach can lead students to be people-pleasers who are guided by no wider purposes than the immediate needs of others close to them. Thus, they find themselves tossed by the waves of those needs with no clear anchor.

Who can save us from the contingencies of self-authored and socially authored lives and give us a stable source of worth, a clear purpose, and a deeper understanding of the good life? We need to understand the purpose we were given by the one who designed us.

PART II

Our Original Identity and Purpose

Being and Bearing God's Image[1]

One of the odd things I find when I interview college students is an answer I get from around 5 percent of students. These students claim that they have a purpose, but they also admit to not knowing what it is. Often, these students will use the language of feelings. They will confess things such as the following:

- "I do feel a defined sense of purpose, but it's more of something that I'm trying to still navigate."
- "I feel like I have my purpose, but ultimately, I don't really know what I'm on this earth for."
- "I think everyone has a life purpose. I think I do have a life purpose. I'm not sure what it is yet."
- "I think I have a sense of purpose, but I don't exactly know what that purpose is."
- "Um, I have a sense of purpose, like it's driven towards something, but what the end goal is, not a hundred percent sure yet."

1. I am indebted to Carmen Joy Imes, *Being God's Image: Why Creation Still Matters* (IVP Academic, 2023) for one part of this phrasing.

Why would students have this idea that they have a purpose but not know what it is?

Even though we have fallen, there is something in the way that God created us that beckons us to recover our original purpose that God gave us from the start. The problem is that through the fall, we lost our direct understanding of that purpose. Thus, we must learn how to recover the exact nature of this purpose.

Authors have written mounds of books to help young people find their purpose or vocation. Unfortunately, these resources often fail to acknowledge that we must all start by recognizing three important realities. First, God gave us all one important purpose or vocation: to be and to bear his image. Second, the reason God has saved us from sin is to fulfill the original purpose for which he designed us. In other words, God's actions toward us are what should motivate us to be and bear his image. Third, we are and become God's image by acquiring his excellencies in particular identities. Part 2 explores the theological foundations for this outlook.

CHAPTER THREE

Who Are You, *Really*?

> So God created humans in his image,
> in the image of God he created them;
> male and female he created them.
>
> —Genesis 1:27 NRSVue

Imagine growing up thinking that you are an orphan. We do not need much help imagining that situation. Many of the delightful stories we love start with an orphan boy or girl who is living without their true parents, or at least one parent, in a difficult situation. Think about Cinderella, Jane Eyre, Harry Potter, Beauty and the Beast, or Tarzan. The parentless or motherless child immediately has our sympathy. Sometimes, though, there is an added dimension. As in the case of Harry Potter, the Beast, or Tarzan, these characters also have a hidden identity that is something vitally important—it holds the key to their whole story. Furthermore, discovering this hidden identity reveals that someone who seems to have no special qualities or even horrific qualities descended from a heroic, noble, or royal lineage.

All of us come into this world in the same predicament. We, too, have been endowed with a secret royal identity that we can discover only through God and God's people. As Genesis 1:27 declares, you are made in God's image. You were not born with the knowledge that God made you in his image. You discover this only through the means of God's revelation, transmitted by God's people.

Unfortunately, even many people who discover and understand that God made them in his image have no understanding of the incredible implications of that reality. For them, it is like being lost in a barren wasteland their whole lives and then suddenly discovering they are among the elite or royalty of Switzerland, one of the most beautiful and wealthiest countries in the world. They have no prior context for understanding what this other, original identity even means. In this chapter, I unpack one of the implications of this bestowed identity. It concerns who can claim this royal title bestowed by God.

Who Is Made in God's Image?

In her book *Mothers, Children, and the Body Politic: Ancient Christianity and the Recovery of Human Dignity*, Nadya Williams tells the story of how in 55 BC Julius Caesar came across two Germanic tribes in what is now the Netherlands. Other Germanic tribes had driven them to that area. Caesar recounted in his campaign log, *Gallic War*, what he did next. His army slaughtered what he estimated were 430,000 helpless men, women, and children (modern-day digging has unearthed the remains of 150,000). According to Caesar, not one Roman soldier died in the process.[1]

While today we would view such an action as genocide, it is only because we live with the belief that all human beings—those outside our tribe, including women, children, the poor, and people with disabilities—are worthwhile and have inherent dignity. People throughout the ancient world did not have that view. Cultures around the globe maintained hierarchical views of human worth and dignity. They believed some people were more important and valuable than others.

First, at the top of the hierarchy were those humans considered valuable in ancient societies—men within the empire who could contribute to military conquest. Thus, women and children were unhelpful beyond

1. Nadya Williams, *Mothers, Children, and the Body Politic: Ancient Christianity and the Recovery of Human Dignity* (IVP Academic, 2024), 115.

their potential to produce or become future warriors. The infirm were particularly problematic. As the historian Gary Ferngren noted,

> There was . . . little sympathy in early Greek literature for the physically impaired or oppressed, an attitude that can be demonstrated to have characterized both popular and official opinion in virtually every period of classical antiquity. Attitudes to the physically defective reflected the belief that health and physical wholeness were essential to human dignity, so much so that life without them was not thought to be worth living. Citizenship, kinship, status, merit, and virtue formed the foundation of claims to the possession of human rights or human worth. Those who lacked them (e.g., orphans, slaves, foundlings, the physically defective, prisoners) had no claim to the rights that they alone guaranteed or even to a recognition of their human worth.[2]

One finds this outlook represented in what Aristotle famously argued in the *Nicomachean Ethics*: "For the person who is terribly ugly, of low birth, or solitary and childless is not really the sort to be happy."[3]

Second, there were those outside of this hierarchy, one's tribe or empire. As we see from Williams's illustration, the ancients considered outsiders as either nonhuman or less than human. As the earlier example illustrates, these groups could be enslaved or wiped out completely. Their lives were worthwhile only as future workers or slaves, nothing more.

Amid this hierarchical understanding of humanity, Genesis 1 declares that God made all humanity in his image (Latin: *imago Dei*). In contrast to the ancient world, this royal title is not something bestowed on a special few. J. Richard Middleton, in his book *The Liberating Image: The Imago Dei in Genesis 1*, helps us understand how radical this declaration was. He points out that in the ancient world, only kings—or occasionally priests—would be given the title of image bearer or likeness of God, and they then mediated the divine to the people they ruled.[4]

In contrast, within Genesis "the imago Dei designates the royal office or calling of human beings as God's representatives and agents in the

2. Gary B. Ferngren, *Medicine and Health Care in Early Christianity* (Johns Hopkins University Press, 2009), 95–96.

3. Aristotle, *Nicomachean Ethics*, trans. and ed. Roger Crisp (Cambridge University Press, 2000), 15.

4. J. Richard Middleton, *The Liberating Image: The Imago Dei in Genesis 1* (Baker Academic, 2005), 26–27.

world, granted authorized power to share in God's rule or administration of the earth's resources and creatures."[5] In other words, God bestowed the title of image bearers on all humans. As Middleton tells us, "The use of *imago Dei* language in Genesis 1 . . . functions to delegitimate any intrinsically hierarchical social structure and affirm the dignity and agency of all humanity."[6]

It is vitally important that we understand these two qualities: dignity and agency. The biblical scholar Carmen Joy Imes helps us by using a couple of different words. She writes, "To be God's image implies kinship. We are God's family. Being God's image involves both kinship and kingship. We are part of the royal family."[7] Both terms are important.

God's Family: Human Dignity and Worth

First, the good news we receive from recognizing this all-important gift from God is that we have a source of dignity, worth, and value that is unchangeable. It is the source of what scholars call *universal worth*—the belief that you and others are all equally created, loved, and valued by God.[8] Thus, your worth is not contingent on successes or failures, virtues or vices. You do not derive universal worth from your accomplishments, being part of a particular tribe, your sense of being better than others, or the contingent evaluations of other humans. Nor is it related to your overall feelings of self-regard. It is simply a reality established by God. The reality that God made all humanity in his image establishes the worth of all individuals. Everyone has dignity.

Thus, unlike finding worth in your appearance, achievements, or others' approval, recognizing and internalizing that God made you in his image means you can know that your worth is not dependent on your temporary natural gifts, relationships, or achievements. As we have seen in the first chapter, young adults usually justify their worth and value through self-authored and socially authored means. Most have not yet

5. Middleton, *Liberating Image*, 27.

6. Middleton, *Liberating Image*, 206.

7. Carmen Joy Imes, *Being God's Image: Why Creation Still Matters* (IVP Academic, 2023), 32.

8. Steven V. Rouse, "Universal Worth: Construct and Scale Development," *Journal of Personality Assessment* 94, no. 1 (2012): 62–72.

proven themselves in the world—their high school achievements and relational capital have taken them only so far—and as the last chapter mentioned, those identities, achievements, or relationships may not carry over after high school since they are based on extrinsic sources that can prove unstable and vary considerably.

The familial identity God bestows on us provides a unique way of establishing our worth. One student I interviewed understood the practical implications: "The fact that I was made in the image of God blows my mind, honestly. And it's not something you think about every day, I guess. But because of that knowledge, I don't really feel like I question, you know, 'Am I worth being alive?'" He recognized that everyone, including himself, has dignity and worth.

Sometimes we forget that the good news of the gospel starts with this teaching. I remember talking to a seminary professor about the topic of evangelism. During the conversation, we both agreed that it is tragic that many familiar presentations of the gospel start with our core problem: We are sinners. They do not start with our original identity and its associated purpose. We are image bearers of God. Yet he shared that a missionary he knew serving the destitute poor in Peru found that he had to begin with Genesis 1 and declare to the poor that they are made in God's image. When I asked him why, he replied, "Because they knew they were sinners. What they lacked was any sense of their human dignity."

In other words, the problem with much of Christian evangelism is that it starts with the second major gift God gave us through Christ (salvation from sin) and does not start by telling everyone about one of God's first gifts to humanity. God bestowed it on us like an inherited familial title. It is also free, just like your own family identity. We have done nothing ourselves to acquire this identity. Furthermore, its meaning comes to us only through God and his revelation.[9]

Part of the Royal Family: Human Agency

Second, the fact that God made us in his image means God granted us agency regarding our relationships with him, with others, and with his world. Middleton observes that this reality means that "all persons

9. For more on the biblical understanding of this concept, see Imes, *Being God's Image*.

have equal access to God simply by being human."[10] In the New Testament, this understanding is amplified by the view that Christ is our high priest (see Hebrews) and is the only mediator that humans need in order to approach God.

Furthermore, the agency of individual humans matters amid this relationship. As Middleton states, "It is ordinary humans (and not some elite class) who are understood to be significant historical actors in the arena of earthly life."[11] A king or queen or some ruling class is not earth's most important historical actor. God tasked every individual with a set of important missions that can be properly understood only if we understand what it means to be made in God's image.

What Exactly Is the Mission of Those in This Royal Family?

The key to answering the question in this heading is understanding the connection between the declaration that humans are made in God's image in Genesis 1:27 and the following benediction to humans in verse 28: "God blessed them and said to them, 'Be fruitful and increase in number; fill the earth and subdue it. Rule over the fish in the sea and the birds in the sky and over every living creature that moves on the ground.'" Middleton summarizes his exposition of the meaning of this connection in this way: "Said one way, humans are like God in exercising royal power on earth. Said in another way, the divine ruler delegated to humans a share in his rule of the earth."[12] Our central purpose is fulfilling this royal function granted to us by God.

Although the rest of this book will explain this function in further detail, this chapter will start by outlining three implications related directly to Genesis 1.

To understand these implications, we must recognize that knowing God and our sub-identities matters immensely. What do I mean by sub-identities? One of the ways we know God is by sub-identities. God is Creator, King, Father, Shepherd, and more, but these terms do not

10. Middleton, *Liberating Image*, 207.
11. Middleton, *Liberating Image*, 204.
12. Middleton, *Liberating Image*, 88.

fully describe God. When describing what it means to understand our meta-identity of being made in God's image, Middleton refers to two sub-identities, God as Ruler and Creator. In the same way, according to Genesis 1, God has designed and commissioned us to take on those functions.

Royal Stewards of God's Creation

First, God gives his royal representatives the power and agency to rule his creation (Gen. 1:28). As Middleton notes, "The *imago Dei* is thus inextricably linked to the gift and responsibility (delegated to humanity at creation) of exercising stewardship over the earth. . . . Humans are entrusted with nothing less than *God's own proper work*, as the creator's authorized representatives on the earth."[13] God has entrusted his whole creation to us—including our own uniquely formed bodies and gifts that God has given us. First Peter 4:10 simply reaffirms this responsibility given in creation: "Like good stewards of the manifold grace of God, serve one another with whatever gift each of you has received" (NRSVue).

Again, I see a particular problem emerge from Christians who neglect this crucial point. They view being a biologist, chemist, or physicist as less spiritual than being a pastor, social worker, or teacher. In other words, they focus only on a certain meaning of Christ's Great Commission given in Matthew 28:18–20 and then think that we help fulfill it only through certain vocations. What they fail to realize is that being a disciple of Christ also involves recovering our originally created purpose. One of our originally created purposes involves exercising God's royal authority, entrusted to us as stewards, over creation.[14]

For example, to become a natural scientist is to search for the secrets the creator of the universe has hidden within creation. It is like joining in a great treasure hunt devised by our Creator and Father. Proverbs 25:2

13. Middleton, *Liberating Image*, 204, 212. Chrysostom and Ambrose also shared this understanding of the image of God as related to dominion.

14. Various Jewish and Christian scholars have argued about whether dominion is the main function of image bearers or if it "results from the divine image but does not comprise it." Jeremy Cohen, *Be Fertile and Increase, Fill the Earth and Master It: The Ancient and Medieval Career of a Biblical Text* (Cornell University Press, 1989), 23. According to either interpretation, however, the responsibility of stewarding God's creation is necessarily related to bearing God's image.

states, "It is the glory of God to conceal a matter; to search out a matter is the glory of kings." Because we are image bearers, our royal calling is to search out and discover God's mysteries.

Creators/Artisans

Second, God made us creators. Just as God is an artisan who created billions of universes, our own natural world, and all humanity, we are to continue in that role by creating other people and culture (human-made creations).[15] One sees this former capacity exercised in Genesis 4:1–2 and this latter capacity exercised immediately in Genesis 2:19–20 when God invites Adam to name the wild animals and birds using words, just as God created using words. Adam thus creates human culture by creating names. Middleton also observes that the Genesis story "recounts the founding of the first city not by God but by a human being (Gen. 4:17) and lists three brothers (Jabal, Jubal, and Tubal-Cain) as the inventors of metallurgy, music, and nomadic livestock herding (4:20–22). . . . Later, Noah is depicted as planting the first vineyard (9:20), and Nimrod is said to be the first warrior (10:8)."[16] The Genesis account celebrates human creativity as part of image bearing. God gives us the privilege of adding to his creation.

This reality has tremendous implications for how we understand the range of careers and professions humans have pursued in the world. I sometimes hear young Christians talk about certain jobs as if they matter only when related to Christ's Great Commission. Thus, an engineer or businessperson is important because they can earn money to give to the church and missions. Again, this outlook totally misses God's first Great Commission given in creation. As divine image bearers, we have been given the privilege of creating just as God creates. That means engineers, entrepreneurs, architects, artisans, filmmakers, authors, and so on are all doing something for which God designed them. They are bearing God's image by creating just as God creates. In J.R.R. Tolkien's words, they are "sub-creators" because they are imitating the creative and imaginative God in whose image we are made.[17]

15. Middleton, *Liberating Image*, 89.
16. Middleton, *Liberating Image*, 217.
17. J. R. R. Tolkien, *Tree and Leaf* (Unwin, 1964), 70.

Additional Sub-Identity Roles

Now, it is important to recognize that this imitation of God's sub-identity roles is extended in other places in Scripture beyond those associated with the image of God in Genesis 1 (although sometimes implicit there). For example, God not only created male and female in his image but also created the identities of husband and wife. Based on that creation, "a man leaves his father and mother and is united to his wife, and they become one flesh" (Gen. 2:24 and repeated by Jesus in Matt. 19:5 and Mark 10:7 and by Paul in Eph. 5:31). Paul also refers to Christ as the husband to the church (Eph. 5:32).

Similarly, just as Christ is the Good Shepherd (John 10:11–18; Heb. 13:20; 1 Pet. 2:25), humans are commanded to shepherd God's flock (Acts 20:28; 1 Pet. 5:2). In addition, just as God is a warrior, we are instructed to wage war against the spiritual forces of darkness (Eph. 6:10–20). God has given us the privilege of emulating his identities and imitating what he does in ways beyond just these two identities established in Genesis 1.

The overall implication of being made in God's image, then, is that like God, we too have numerous sub-identity roles in which God commanded us to seek excellence. We are to be excellent humans, men or women, husbands or wives, sons or daughters, neighbors, friends, citizens, and a host of other identities we take on or have bestowed on us. Unfortunately, we used our agency and royal commission to try to alter God's plan for us.

How the Fall Defaced the *Imago Dei*

The fall described in Genesis 3 and its influence on humans as image bearers of God has been an important and central conversation among Christians. Understanding the implications of the fall for human identity helps one understand what it means to be made in God's image at a deeper level.

Claiming That Humans Lost the Image of God

Often throughout history, Christians have given Satan and sin too much credit. That is certainly the case when it comes to how Christians have understood the effects of the fall as it relates to their status as image bearers. A few wayward Christian thinkers throughout history claimed that the fall destroyed the image of God in humans.[18] One such thinker declared, "We had by sin lost *the Image of God*, and thereby all gracious acceptance with him."[19]

The problem with this view is that it is not consistent with Scripture. God declared in his covenant with Noah, after the fall and the destruction of most of humanity through the flood, "Whoever sheds human blood, by humans shall their blood be shed; for in the image of God has God made mankind" (Gen. 9:6). In other words, God predicated this moral instruction in this case on the fact that, even after the fall, humans are still to be understood as being made in his image. This understanding applies to all humans, no matter what their beliefs or actions.

Fortunately, most thinkers throughout Christian history took this more biblical view. Church fathers such as Ambrose and Augustine taught that while the image was "deformed and discolored," the image itself was not lost.[20] The seventeenth-century writer John Weldon uses terminology from the art of sculpting to provide a helpful description of how sin influences the image: "'Tis true, our sins may deface this Image within our souls, however they can't utterly blast it; for it is an inherent property in the wicked as well as in the just."[21] The difference being the righteous "are a lively image of God, whereas the wicked are

18. Two scholars who held this view were John Wycliffe and Richard FitzRalph. Anthony Pagden and J. Lawrence claim, "Their account accepts that man is made in the likeness of God; however, they also argue that this likeness and the dominion consequent to it are corrupted by sin, the conclusion being: 'the image of God is not in the sinner, hence the sinner cannot have such dominion [what I label stewardship].'" F. de Vitoria, "On the American Indians," in *Political Writings*, ed. Anthony Pagden and J. Lawrence (Cambridge University Press, 1991), 84.

19. John Owen, *The Declaration of the Glorious Mystery of the Person of Christ, God and Man* (1679), 287. See Suzanne McDonald, "Historical and Theological Studies: The Pneumatology of the Lost Image in John Owen," *The Westminster Theological Journal* 71, no. 2 (2009): 323–35. McDonald points out that Owen was "distinctive even within his own tradition for his evident reluctance to speak of any remnant of the image outside the elect" (329).

20. Gerald Boersma, *Augustine's Early Theology of Image: A Study in the Development of Pro-Nicene Theology* (Oxford University Press, 2016), 261; Matthew Drever, *Image, Identity, and the Forming of the Augustinian Soul* (Oxford University Press, 2013); Luigi Gioia, *The Theological Epistemology of Augustine's De Trinitate* (Oxford University Press, 2008).

21. John Weldon, *The Divine Pedagogue* (1692), 1.

indeed a sort of an image of God."[22] In other words, much like vandals throughout history have often tried to deface statues that humans have created, sin and Satan merely defaced God's wonderful creation. They did not destroy our fundamental identity. Despite our fallen condition, all of us are still made in God's image.

Destroying the Individual

One major way the fall defaced humanity was by destroying the connection between individual human dignity and the image of God. It is hard for us to believe today, but early Western and Eastern philosophical thought placed little emphasis on the individual person and a person's will apart from their social roles in society. We find throughout ancient civilizations, whether in the Middle East, China, or India, that individuals were not valuable in and of themselves. Instead, a person's value was determined by their social role, such as being a warrior, a woman, a slave, a child, or a member of a particular caste.

Furthermore, a person's identity was completely defined by these social roles. For example, Confucian scholars observed of early Chinese thought, "No-thing or no-body has an *essence*, but each can be defined only 'correlationally,' at any given time, with differing relations holding at other times; we are both benefactors and beneficiaries of our friends, neighbors, lovers, colleagues, and so forth, dependent on specific circumstances."[23] This reality is why banishment was such a terrible punishment. Being cut off from one's tribe and one's other relationships destroyed that person's identity. In a sense, that person no longer existed. There was no such thing as individual dignity, value, worth, or rights.

22. Weldon, *Divine Pedagogue*, 1. Similarly, George Trosse, an English minister, wrote in 1692 "of that image of God which was instamped upon Man plainly and fully at first; and remains imperfectly and obscurely in all men; and is restored to the saints in their regeneration, and is increased in them in their progressive sanctification." George Trosse, *The Lord's Day Vindicated or First Day of the Week the Christian Sabbath* (Samuel Clement, 1692), 22.

23. Confucius, *The Analects of Confucius: A Philosophical Translation*, ed. Robert T. Ame and Henry Rosemont Jr. (Ballantine Books, 1999), 24. See also Roger T. Ames, *Human Becomings: Theorizing Persons for Confucian Role Ethics* (State University of New York Press, 2021).

This view also extended to human agency. Middleton notes that ancient Near Eastern stories often attributed human accomplishments, such as names or building cities, to the gods. Humans, especially in ancient and contemporary animistic tribal cultures, were also considered subject to the whims of natural forces and spirits beyond their control. They downplayed human agency. As a result, we as humans focused less on stewarding God's creation and instead began to fear it and to worship our own creations. As Romans 1:22–23 describes it, "Although they claimed to be wise, they became fools and exchanged the glory of the immortal God for images made to look like a mortal human being and birds and animals and reptiles." One dimension of the glory of the immortal God that we humans lost was remembering that he made us in his image.

The Law and Restraining the Fall

Against this backdrop, one can understand more fully God's later prohibition against images. Now, it is always helpful to remember what Jesus reminded us in Mark 10:5: "It was because your hearts were hard that Moses wrote you this law." Thus, the law does not fully capture God's original intentions outlined in creation. Instead, just as God's law prohibiting divorce was not God's original intention for marriage, the law against making idols resulted from failing to live up to God's original ideals—recognizing humans and not statues as image bearers of God.

With this background in mind, we can understand the first two commandments from Exodus 20:3–6: "You shall have no other gods before me. You shall not make for yourself an image in the form of anything in heaven above or on the earth beneath or in the waters below. You shall not bow down to them or worship them; for I, the LORD your God, am a jealous God, punishing the children for the sin of the parents to the third and fourth generation of those who hate me, but showing love to a thousand generations of those who love me and keep my commandments."

Middleton argues that we need to see these prohibitions as addressing how the entire system of the creation and worship of idols in the ancient world undermined God's intention for humans to fulfill their purpose as image bearers. First, it undermined human dignity, surrendering human worth and agency to human creations and an unequal system of priest-mediated worship. Second, idol worship gave up, and still gives up, the human agency God bestowed on us to create. Instead, the idol worshipers "give over their fundamental human calling to mediate God's power on earth in significant cultural innovation by projecting this calling onto blocks of wood and stone."[24] Our fallenness results in our giving up and actually rejecting the gifts that God has given us by creating us as his image bearers. As Middleton states, "Idolatry is part and parcel of a larger priest-controlled social system that disempowers ordinary people by robbing them of both access to God and significant agency in the world."[25] Thus, God himself would need to come show us what it means to bear his image in human form. The next chapter explores what Christ revealed to us about what it means to be and to bear God's image.

24. Middleton, *Liberating Image*, 208.
25. Middleton, *Liberating Image*, 209.

CHAPTER FOUR

Being and Bearing God's Image

What Christ Taught Us

The Son is the image of the invisible God.

—Colossians 1:15a

Imagine that an artistic masterpiece has been defaced by someone who simply delights in destroying the beauty of creation. You want to restore the piece but do not know where to begin. You know what not to do and have an idea about the rules and principles to follow so as not to further damage the piece. In addition, you have some ideas about the purpose of this artistic treasure. Yet, not only do you not have the expertise for the restoration, but you do not even have a picture of what the prior masterpiece looked like.

Now, of course, you could try to restore the masterpiece on your own without the necessary skills or knowledge. That is what happened to a fresco of Jesus named *Ecce Homo* (Latin: "Behold the Man") created by Elías García Martínez. An eighty-two-year-old parishioner of the church where the art was located, the Sanctuary of Mercy in Borja,

Spain, tried to restore the work. The result, as you can see below, was tragically comical.[1]

Figure 4.1. The original *Ecce Homo* fresco of Jesus by the nineteenth-century painter Elías García Martínez

Public Domain / Wikimedia Commons

Figure 4.2. The "restored" version by Cecilia Giménez, a parishioner in her eighties

Alberto Paredes / Alamy

Now, imagine if the original creator of the artwork had engaged in the restoration. At the most important level, we do not have to imagine. God designed us to be his image bearers. However, since we defaced that image, we needed God to come and not simply save us from our sin (although that was our fundamental need to restore our relationship with him). We also needed our original Creator to demonstrate to us anew what it means to be "the image of the invisible God" in human form (Col. 1:15). In Christ, we find all of God's original intentions for humanity fulfilled. Christ supplies us with all that we lost from the fall by giving us the knowledge, restored relationship with

1. Ruge Ferreira, "So Bad That It's Good: 5 Worst Art Restorations," *Daily Art Magazine*, April 1, 2025, https://www.dailyartmagazine.com/worst-artworks-restorations/. See also Raphael Minder, "Despite Good Intentions, a Fresco in Spain Is Ruined," *New York Times*, August 24, 2012, https://www.nytimes.com/2012/08/24/world/europe/botched-restoration-of-ecce-homo-fresco-shocks-spain.html.

God, and power—through the Holy Spirit—to recover our originally created purpose.

In this chapter, I will focus on two major things Christ supplied beyond saving us from our sin. First, Christ reaffirmed our individual human dignity and agency that we already possessed as image bearers of God. Second, Christ revealed *how* we are to engage in our core rulership purposes. As Stanley Grenz puts it, "Jesus came to fulfill our human vocation as the *imago Dei* . . . we cannot see God's purposes for creation except in relationship to Jesus, who as the *imago Dei* in fulfillment of the human vocation is the cosmic Christ."[2] Specifically, Christ, as the fulfiller of our original vocation, demonstrated something new that we would not have needed in creation but that we do need in a fallen world. He showed the most important character qualities, fruits of the Spirit, or virtues to acquire and demonstrate in a fallen world as we go about fulfilling our original role as stewards of creation. These are virtues that require suffering to reverse the fall.

The Reaffirmation of Individual Human Dignity and Worth

First, let us contemplate what Christ's incarnation and life mean for individual worth and dignity. As the last chapter mentioned, one of the tragic effects of the fall is that ancient societies judged human worth based on one's role in society. To be poor, a woman, a child, a person with leprosy, or a physically disabled individual was to be of less worth. Christ directly challenged that fallen understanding of human worth in two ways.

Our Bodily Worth

Christ affirmed the value of all humanity by becoming human. As the Christmas hymn "O Holy Night" declares, we lay in sin "Till he appear'd and the soul felt its worth."[3] Yet we must recognize that Christ did not simply affirm our soul's worth. He affirmed the worth of whole human persons, including the worth of our physical bodies.

2. Stanley Grenz, "Jesus as the *Imago Dei*: Image-of-God Christology and the Non-Linear Linearity of Theology," *JETS* 47 (2004): 625, 627.

3. Adolphe Adam, "Christmas Hymn; O Holy Night" (W. F. Sudds, 1883).

Christ's affirmation of human bodies can be found in the Fourth Gospel, which contains a different Christmas story: "And the Word became flesh and lived among us" (John 1:14a NRSVue). Without an understanding of both Greek and Gnostic thought at the time these words were written, it is difficult to understand how revolutionary this statement is. To many hearers of this Gospel who were influenced by certain kinds of Greek thought, the body was vile, broken, and sinful. Only the mind and soul were of eternal worth and value.[4]

Christ becoming flesh countered this mistaken teaching. Those with deformed, mutilated, or different bodies (e.g., those who are blind, deaf, mentally disabled, physically handicapped, lame, leprous, and even demon-possessed) all have equal worth. All for whom Christ died have tremendous worth in God's eyes. To denigrate others' dignity, including their bodies, is to denigrate glorious image bearers of God (James 3:9).

Furthermore, Christ's physical body provided the instrument of our salvation. As Colossians 1:21–22 reminds us, "Once you were alienated from God and were enemies in your minds because of your evil behavior. But now he has reconciled you by *Christ's physical body* through death to present you holy in his sight, without blemish and free from accusation" (emphasis added). Or as we remember the words of Christ whenever we celebrate the Lord's Supper, "This is my *body* given for you" (Luke 22:19, emphasis added). A human body became the greatest sacrifice in the history of time.

We Are More Than Social Identities

Christ also reaffirmed our worth not simply by taking human form and sacrificing his physical body but also through how he lived. Over and over in the Gospels, we see Christ elevate a person above their social role and place them in a transcendent story that was larger than any simple sub-identity. These individuals are not simply a young peasant girl, a person with leprosy, a member of another tribe (i.e., a Samaritan or Roman centurion), or even a Pharisee. Each one of us is the child of a king with a royal inheritance and role to play. Even though humanity

4. For more on this topic, see Perry L. Glanzer and Julia Hejduk, "The Body in the Biblical Narrative: Foundations," in *Stewarding Our Bodies: A Vision for Christian Student Affairs* (Abilene Christian University Press, 2023), 17–32.

was alienated from God, everyone can and should once again access this inheritance that Christ brought back to us.

Christ's affirmation of the individual is revealed through the application and extension of Jewish and Christian thought about what it means to be made in the image of God. In contrast to both early Greek and Chinese thinkers, Christ and then his followers maintained that individuals were more than their social roles and were gifted with an individual will. Thus, throughout Christ's ministry, one finds Christ calling individuals to follow him and not simply a tribe. Furthermore, he points out that one's social roles, whether being an outcast, a woman, a slave, a widow, a gentile, or even a son or daughter, are not one's fundamental identity. All humans, no matter their station in life, are image bearers of the triune God. One finds this point implicit in Christ's teaching:

> Then the King will say to those on his right, "Come, you who are blessed by my Father; take your inheritance, the kingdom prepared for you since the creation of the world. For I was hungry and you gave me something to eat, I was thirsty and you gave me something to drink, I was a stranger and you invited me in, I needed clothes and you clothed me, I was sick and you looked after me, I was in prison and you came to visit me." Then the righteous will answer him, "Lord, when did we see you hungry and feed you, or thirsty and give you something to drink? When did we see you a stranger and invite you in, or needing clothes and clothe you? When did we see you sick or in prison and go to visit you?" The King will reply, "Truly I tell you, whatever you did for one of the least of these brothers and sisters of mine, you did for me." (Matt. 25:34–40)

The least among humanity is comparable in their intrinsic worth to the King.

Furthermore, all humans are not only intrinsically worthwhile but also individually able to repent and restore their relationship with God. Indeed, what some considered privileged identities, such as being a Jew, a Pharisee, rich, or a son/daughter (Matt. 10:35–37), could be hurdles that need to be overcome while following him to this restoration (Matt. 19:16–24).

The apostles also point to how the new identity that Christ has provided us reorders how we think about the value of our previous social identities. For example, Paul makes clear in Philippians that all of his positive identities of privilege—"circumcised on the eighth day, of the people of Israel, of the tribe of Benjamin, a Hebrew of Hebrews; in regard to the law, a Pharisee" (Phil. 3:5)—are now worthless compared to "the surpassing worth of knowing Christ Jesus my Lord" (v. 8). Everyone, no matter how lacking in ability or earthly autonomy (e.g., slaves and children), can now freely choose to follow Christ and find their righteousness in him.

The apostles made clear that the gospel message was for everyone and not just a particular elite. This change in audience was groundbreaking. Larry Siedentop observes that Paul's message of salvation for all "overturns the assumption on which ancient thinking had hitherto rested, the assumption of natural inequality."[5] He goes on to note, "For Paul, belief in the Christ makes possible the emergence of a primary role shared equally by all . . . while conventional social roles—whether of father, daughter, official, priest, or slave become secondary in relation to that primary role. To this primary role an indefinite number of social roles may or may not be added as attributes of a subject, but they no longer define the subject."[6]

This primary role is that we are God's children—an identity mentioned in most of Paul's letters (Rom. 8:16–21; Gal. 3:26; 4:7; Eph. 5:8; Phil. 2:15; 1 Thess. 5:5) as well as John's writings (John 1:12–13; 1 John 3:1–2). Indeed, the phrase "born again" used in John 3:3 harks back to the original creation story. Christians can start over again as children of God who are made in God's image and fulfill their original responsibilities as image bearers of God.

Siedentop observes that this new identity not only elevates the individual but gives people particular moral responsibilities: "Now, the identity of individuals is no longer exhausted by the social roles they happen to occupy. A gap opens between individuals and the roles they occupy. That gap marks the advent of the new freedom, freedom of conscience. But it also introduces moral obligations that follow from recognizing that all humans are children of God."[7] The moral obligations are not only our rulership obligations discussed in the last chapter. Christ also shows us

5. Larry Siedentop, *Inventing the Individual: The Origins of Western Liberalism* (Belknap, 2014), 59.

6. Siedentop, *Inventing the Individual*, 62.

7. Siedentop, *Inventing the Individual*, 61–62.

the rulership virtues we need to demonstrate as we go about being and bearing God's image in a fallen world.

A Key Component of Creativity and Stewardship: How to Reverse the Fall

Beginning in Genesis 12 with Abraham and then throughout the rest of the Old Testament, we find how God revealed to the people of Israel how they were supposed to reverse the fall before the time of the Messiah. They were to look to God to save them from slavery, enemies, and so on, and then live a life of gratitude for God's redemption by being a holy people, a people set apart for God.

When discussing the priests who offer sacrifices to God for sin, Leviticus 21:8b declares, "Consider them holy, because I the LORD am holy—I who make you holy." But the Israelites were not simply to acknowledge that God set them apart and made them holy; they were to participate in this endeavor as well. Thus, one of the only passages in the Old Testament law to rely on an appeal to imitating God says in Leviticus 19:2b, "Be holy because I, the LORD your God, am holy." The key elements to being holy involved following the Old Testament law.

Nevertheless, the purpose of the law was not to save Israel. As Paul says in Galatians, "It was added because of transgressions until the Seed to whom the promise referred had come. . . . So the law was our guardian until Christ came that we might be justified by faith" (3:19, 24). Striving after holiness would make them conscious of sin and their need for blood sacrifice in order to be rightly related to God.

Through Christ, we find God's redemptive message expanded to all who bear his image (and even to the whole natural world). Just as God saved and set apart Israel to be a blessing to all nations (Gen. 12:3), God, through Christ, reverses the fall for all of us. He destroyed the devil's work (1 John 3:8) and became the final atoning blood sacrifice for our sin (Rom. 3:25).

Nonetheless, as theologian Stanley Grenz said, "Understanding the Christian message as centering on God's work in remedying the human sin problem through Christ's death . . . is not the whole story."[8] The rest

8. Grenz, "Jesus as the *Imago Dei*," 617.

of the story is that through Christ, we can be born again so that we once again fulfill our purpose to be and bear God's image. Or as Grenz writes, "The NT presents Jesus as the true image of God, who through his mission on God's behalf—especially in the cross and resurrection—reveals the divine reality and thereby completes the vocation of humankind."[9]

In addition, Christ does something more that is vitally important. Just as God invited us to steward his creation, pursue our own creative endeavors (culture), and mediate between God and creation, Christ calls us to join with him and extend this rule concerning all fallen humanity and creation. We are called once again to steward Christ's new kingdom, extend its rule, and bring God's message of salvation and the renewed kingdom to all humanity. It is important to recognize that Christ demonstrated how these moral responsibilities must be carried out. In other words, Christ clearly shows us *how* to go about fulfilling our purpose in a fallen world.

Recovering the Image of God

Christ appearing in human flesh not only revealed to us the glorious dignity of humanity. His life also became the most powerful teaching lesson ever. Christ taught us how to bear God's image in a fallen world. We needed this lesson since after we place our faith in Christ's saving work, bearing God's image becomes our primary end. Indeed, as the biblical scholar N. T. Wright observed, "The whole New Testament insists that the point of Christian living is the remaking of humans in God's image."[10]

Consider, for example, Colossians 3. Paul states, "Do not lie to each other, since you have taken off your old self with its practices and have put on the new self, which is being renewed in knowledge in the image of its Creator" (vv. 9–10). Here, Paul reminds Christians that the new self is really the originally created self—our restored image. Next, he reaffirms the individual dignity that is bestowed by this title: "Here there

9. Grenz, "Jesus as the *Imago Dei*," 621.

10. N. T. Wright, *After You Believe: Why Christian Character Matters* (HarperOne, 2010), 251.

is no Gentile or Jew, circumcised or uncircumcised, barbarian, Scythian, slave or free, but Christ is all, and is in all" (v. 11). Paul is simply reminding his readers once again what Jesus showed us. Our most important identity is that we are image bearers of God and now sons and daughters of the King.

Second, Paul mentions the clothing that we were originally meant to acquire in the garden of Eden (versus the clothing we acquired from God due to the fall). We were to bear God's image by acquiring and demonstrating his virtues: "Therefore, as God's chosen people, holy and dearly loved, clothe yourselves with compassion, kindness, humility, gentleness and patience. Bear with each other and forgive one another if any of you has a grievance against someone. Forgive as the Lord forgave you. And over all these virtues put on love, which binds them all together in perfect unity" (vv. 12–14).

I have used the word *virtues* to describe what we should recover.[11] It helps to look at Scripture to understand the expansive nature of what this includes. Consider 2 Peter 1:3–7 (RSV), in which we are told,

> His [God's] divine power has granted to us all things that pertain to life and godliness, through the knowledge of him who called us to his own glory and *excellence* [*aretē*], by which he has granted to us his precious and very great promises, that through these you may escape from the corruption that is in the world because of passion, and become partakers of the divine nature. For this very reason make every effort to supplement your faith with *virtue* [*aretē*], and virtue with knowledge, and knowledge with self-control, and self-control with steadfastness, and steadfastness with godliness, and godliness with brotherly affection, and brotherly affection with love. (emphasis added)

We are called to bear God's image or be "partakers of the divine nature" by being excellent in the same way that God is excellent.

11. Virtues are "(a) dispositional, (b) deep-seated (c) habits (d) that contribute to flourishing and (e) that produce activities with the following three features: they are (f) done well, (g) not done poorly, and (h) in accordance with the right motivation and reason." Julliette L. Ratchford, Timothy Pawl, Anne Jeffrey, and Sarah A. Schnitker, "What Is Virtue? Using Philosophy to Refine Psychological Definition and Operationalization," *Philosophical Psychology* 37, no. 8 (2024): 2607, https://doi.org/10.1080/09515089.2023.2203157.

In the New International Version, the English translation of *aretē* in both cases is "goodness." Thus, one can see that *aretē* can be and is translated in three interchangeable ways: *excellence*, *virtue*, and *goodness*. It is the same Greek word that thinkers such as Homer, Plato, and Aristotle used for excellence or virtue. For contemporary readers, I would argue that it is better to use the word *excellence* because it expands our understanding and keeps us from thinking of image bearing as some narrow, moral activity.

Unusually, Wikipedia provides a helpful understanding here: "*Arete* (Ancient Greek: ἀρετή, romanized: *aretḗ*) is a concept in ancient Greek thought that, in its most basic sense, refers to 'excellence' of any kind—especially a person or thing's 'full realization of potential or inherent function.' The term may also refer to excellence in 'moral virtue.'"[12] In other words, *aretē* refers to more than simply moral excellence, although it includes that. Put simply, the Bible calls Christians to be excellent because God is excellent.

It is also important to recognize where *aretē* or excellence falls in the list Peter provides. It comes immediately after faith and right before knowledge. Why is that? We must clarify the excellence we seek before we start pursuing knowledge. After all, there is plenty of knowledge we could gain, but only some of it will help us acquire and participate in God's excellence. Think about a course that simply explores the topic of friendship or marriage. It can provide you plenty of knowledge about those subjects, but that would be different from a course focusing on being an excellent friend or spouse. When you pursue excellence, it narrows the range of knowledge you need.

Interestingly, a medieval Christian thinker, Anselm, coined a phrase that is heard quite often among Christians in higher education: "faith seeking understanding."[13] In reality the phrase does not follow the pattern from 2 Peter 1. A more biblically faithful phrase would be "faith seeking excellence (and then understanding)."

12. Wikipedia, "*Arete*," last modified October 17, 2025, 19:37 (UTC), https://en.wikipedia.org/wiki/Arete.

13. Latin: "*fides quaerens intellectum*." See Anselm, *Monologion; and, Proslogion: With the Replies of Gaunilo and Anselm*, trans. Thomas Williams (Hackett, 1995), 93.

The Relationship Between Being and Bearing God's Image

We have seen that our original dignity and worth as image bearers was already established before participating in God's excellence. And as Carmen Joy Imes has articulated, we are both to be and to become God's image.[14] To help understand the dynamic, consider what we observe in marriage. In the marriage service, a person becomes a husband or wife by participating in a covenantal ceremony before God, who joins us together. Notice that Jesus says of this marriage that God joins us together (Mark 10:9). It is not a result of our work.

Once married, these two individuals take on two new identities first created and bestowed by God—that of husband and of wife (Gen. 2:24–25). These are bestowed identities just like that of being made in God's image or being a man or a woman (Gen. 1:26). To call oneself a husband or wife is to identify with a long tradition of marriage, especially marriage as understood through the biblical narrative. In this story, marriage is an institution established by God in Genesis 1 with particular rules (e.g., "You shall not commit adultery," Exod. 20:14; Matt. 5:27), virtues (e.g., Christlike agape love, Eph. 5:25–28), and practices (e.g., Mark 10:7–8; 1 Cor. 7:5).

Still, there is a difference between simply being a husband and seeking to be an excellent husband like Christ is to the church. Furthermore, simply because I follow rules ("Do not commit adultery") and practices ("Forsake all others") does not make me an excellent husband. I know plenty of husbands and wives who have not committed adultery but have miserable marriages. What makes anyone an excellent husband or wife is practicing particular Christlike virtues. Indeed, acquiring God's virtues is the primary way Scripture encourages us to imitate the triune God.

The Substance of God's Excellence

So, what would it mean to fulfill one's purpose to be an image bearer of God by acquiring Christ's virtues, or as Romans 8:29 states it, "to be conformed to the image of his Son"? A basic starting point would

14. Carmen Joy Imes, *Being God's Image: Why Creation Still Matters* (IVP Academic, 2023).

be to draw on various lists of virtues mentioned in the Bible as character qualities or virtues of the triune God, in whose image we are made (Col. 3 contains one of them). I have listed four of the most well-known biblical lists (see table 4.1).

Here's the first thing we must recognize: As an image bearer of God, you are designed to clothe yourself with and exhibit all these virtues. Yes, we are sinful, but that is not our original identity. Christ has crucified that old self on the cross and given us a new self that reflects our true purpose. In addition, Christ showed us who we were originally designed to be and gave us the Holy Spirit to empower us to live out these virtues. We are not simply trying to work up the power to acquire virtue through our own willpower. We need the help of the Holy Spirit.

Table 4.1

The Prioritized Christian Virtues

Theological Virtues (1 Cor. 13)	Fruit of the Spirit (Gal. 5:22–23)	Colossians 3:12–17	God's Virtues We Are Specifically Told to Imitate
Agape Love	Agape Love	Agape Love	Agape Love (Eph. 5:1–2)
Faith	Faithfulness		
Hope			
	Joy		
	Peace	Peace	
	Patience	Patience	
	Kindness	Kindness	
	Goodness		
	Gentleness	Gentleness	
	Self-Control		
			Acceptance (Rom. 15:7)
		Forgiveness	Forgiveness (Col. 3:13)
		Holy	Holiness (1 Pet. 1:15–16)
		Humility	Humility (Phil. 2:1–11)
			Mercy (Luke 6:36)
			Servant Leadership (John 13:14)
			Endure Suffering for Good (Heb. 12:1–3)

Now, this is not an exhaustive list of Christian virtues mentioned in the Bible. For example, courage, justice, and wisdom are just a few of the many other biblical virtues that are prioritized throughout Scripture. Yet these three virtues have also been emphasized by pagan Greek and Roman thinkers. Thus, I think it is important to focus on those character qualities of the triune God that have been particularly elevated and emphasized by Christ and the apostles.

These virtues are unique in that they are emphasized by Christian communities. If you want evidence of this fact, consider the list of sixty-six virtues I discovered when I examined character education laws in the United States. Not surprisingly, I found only two of the virtues mentioned in this table on the list of sixty-six virtues (kindness and self-control).[15] The virtues that Christ and the apostles emphasized in the New Testament are not normally prized by those who have not become Christians or studied the New Testament.

Why are these virtues unique? The reason is that they consider the fallen world and the habitual actions required to deal with sin. For example, forgiveness is a virtue that was not needed in Eden. It is necessary, however, in a fallen world. Unfortunately, humans without Christ often fail to recognize the importance of this virtue.

I can attest to this point from my own research. For my dissertation, I interviewed over one hundred teachers after the fall of the Soviet Union who had taught communist ethics previously and were presently learning about Christian ethics. One question I asked them was a simple comparison question: How are communist ethics different than Christian ethics? One startling truth they shared was that communist ethics never taught them about the redemptive virtue of forgiveness. For example, Larissa claimed, "Communist ideology never taught us to ask for forgiveness."[16] Olga echoed this point: "We weren't taught to forgive; thus, we never knew what forgiveness is or never knew how to forgive."[17]

This new teaching had a profound personal influence on teachers. Katerina shared what Christian ethics had taught her:

15. Perry L. Glanzer and Andrew J. Milson, "Legislating the Good: A Survey and Evaluation of Contemporary Character Education Legislation," *Educational Policy* 20, no. 3 (2006): 525–50. Forgiveness was also found in only one state—Arizona.

16. This example and the following other examples are taken from Perry L. Glanzer, *The Quest for Russia's Soul: Evangelicals and Moral Education in Post-Communist Russia* (Baylor University Press, 2002).

17. Glanzer, *Quest for Russia's Soul*, 97.

> I have learned to forgive people. I have been taught to forgive people. It's a very good feature. When you forgive people, it's a process. In the Russian language we have such phrase as a stone fall down from yourself—I don't know if you have such an expression in English. You feel such a relief when you forgive. And I study and I learn to forgive only in my Bible study classes. I wasn't such a person before I become a Christian. Shame upon me, but I got revenge before becoming a Christian. I got revenge. And now I can't do this.[18]

Teachers also perceived that this unique virtue of forgiveness made a difference in how other ethical issues were handled. Under communism, as a teacher from St. Petersburg described, the fear of making mistakes and being punished penetrated the system to such a degree that people lied to cover their mistakes:

> Christian morality admits that each person has the right to make the mistake of sin, but the point is how she or he will live after this sin. Will she or he admit this or confess, or will [he or she] keep on in this sin? So Christian morals, as opposed to communist morals, doesn't state the necessity of lying. You don't have to lie, either to yourself or to anyone. If you make a mistake, be open about it, admit this, and try to correct it rather than hide it or wait for punishment or hide it with new mistakes or sins.[19]

This teacher believed that the lack of an ethic of forgiveness contributed to communism's culture of lying.

Teachers also shared about the difficulty in teaching forgiveness to their students who resisted this new idea. One teacher named Vladimir recalled experiencing opposition: "They say, 'I can't forgive this person, I must take revenge.'" Nevertheless, occasionally the lesson of forgiveness would break through to the students. Maria shared:

> I remember one lesson . . . I ask[ed] everybody, what value is most valuable to you. What feature of your friend is the most valuable for you, . . . and most of them said, I will never forgive a betrayer. It was the most [common] definition of a good friendship. One small boy, his name is George,

18. Glanzer, *Quest for Russia's Soul*, 97.
19. Glanzer, *Quest for Russia's Soul*, 98.

> he said, "I can forgive if he'll betray me. I can do it, because if he's my friend, I can do it." It was so touching. And I said, "You George are like Jesus because Jesus forgives. Peter betrayed him three times and he did forgive, because if you are a good Christian, you can try to forgive even your friend." That was a very special moment in our classroom because they did understand something.[20]

It is interesting to note how the students shared an Aristotelian conception of friendship as opposed to a Christian understanding of forgiveness. Alasdair MacIntyre wrote, "Aristotle in considering the nature of friendship had concluded that a good man could not be the friend of a bad man."[21] Thus, Aristotle's universe omits the conception of love for the sinner. In contrast, the Christian narrative celebrates it, as did this Russian teacher who had recently converted to Christianity.

Christians understand forgiveness as one of the most glorious virtues—one that is central to our narrative, as Good Friday reminds us. On that dark day, according to the Gospel of Luke, Jesus's final two acts involved forgiveness. Some of his final words in that Gospel are a prayer asking God, "Father, forgive them, for they do not know what they are doing" (Luke 23:34a). Immediately after, we read about Jesus's promise to the repentant thief, who requests, "Jesus, remember me when you come into your kingdom," to which Jesus replied with glorious words of forgiveness, "Truly I tell you, today you will be with me in paradise" (Luke 23:42, 43). In each of these cases, Christ's forgiveness required both suffering and giving up power in order to reverse the fall. Our forgiveness often requires the same.

This pattern is true with almost all of Christ's redemptive virtues. Agape love requires sacrifice for others' well-being, forgiveness requires no longer holding someone's sin against them, and humility involves overcoming the deadly vice of pride. Consider how Paul, in Philippians 2, asks us to demonstrate Christ's humility and sacrificial love to one another:

20. Glanzer, *Quest for Russia's Soul*, 99.

21. Alasdair MacIntyre, *After Virtue*, 2nd ed. (University of Notre Dame Press, 1984), 149–50.

> In your relationships with one another, have the same mindset as
> Christ Jesus:
> Who, being in very nature God,
> did not consider equality with God something to be used to
> his own advantage;
> rather, he made himself nothing
> by taking the very nature of a servant,
> being made in human likeness.
> And being found in appearance as a man,
> he humbled himself
> by becoming obedient to death—
> even death on a cross! (vv. 5–8)

All these virtues require us to give up our position of power (e.g., acceptance, humility, servant leadership) or having something against someone (e.g., mercy, forgiveness).

Of course, everyone hates suffering. We instinctively try to avoid it or fight it wherever and whenever we can. But there is a certain kind of suffering that, as Christians, we must both recognize and sometimes even embrace as an essential part of the Christian life if we are to bear God's image as Christ did for us. Chapters 11 and 12 will outline the nature of this suffering in more detail. For the next part, however, I want to point out how the two emphases that Christ communicated regarding the image of God—our intrinsic worth and our need to acquire God's virtues—have led to moral progress throughout history that we now celebrate.

PART III

The Historical Consequences of Recognizing That All Humans Are Made in God's Image

In the middle of the fifth century, Theodoret of Cyrus, a Christian bishop and theologian, related a story about the Christian Roman Emperor Theodosius (AD 347–395), who had exacted a new tribute from the people in the empire due to numerous wars. As a result, residents in Antioch (located in present-day Syria) protested this new tribute by pulling down a bronze statue of the emperor's recently deceased wife, Placilla, dragging it throughout the city.

After hearing about this incident, the emperor threatened to destroy the city. When the commissioners bringing the emperor's threats arrived at the city, according to Theodoret, "the whole population shuddered in consternation."[1] There was a monk named Macedonius, however, who

1. Theodoret of Cyrus, "The Ecclesiastical History," trans. Blomfield Jackson, in *Nicene and Post-Nicene Fathers*, 2nd series, vol. 3, ed. Philip Schaff and Henry Wace (Christian Literature, 1892), 205.

lived in the nearby mountains "night and day offering up pure prayers to the Saviour of all."[2] He traveled to town, came to the commissioners, and asked them to dismount: "At the sight of a little old man, clad in common rags, they were at first indignant, but some of those who were conducting them informed them of the high character of Macedonius, and then they sprang from their horses, caught hold of his knees, and asked his pardon."[3] Macedonius, then "urged on by divine wisdom," requested the following:

> Say, dear sirs, to the emperor, you are not only an emperor, you are also a man. Bethink you, therefore, not only of your sovereignty, but also of your nature. You are a man, and you reign over your fellow men. Now the nature of man is formed after the image and likeness of God. Do not, therefore, thus savagely and cruelly order the massacre of God's image, for by punishing His image you will anger the Maker. Think how you are acting thus in your wrath for the sake of a brazen image. Now all who are endued with reason know how far a lifeless image is inferior to one alive and gifted with soul and sense. Take into account, too, that for one image of bronze we can easily make many more. Even you yourself cannot make one single hair of the slain.[4]

According to Theodoret, this theological appeal to the emperor, based on the fact that humans are made in God's image, "quenched the flame of his [Theodosius's] rage."[5]

I rarely find students who understand how important it is to emphasize the truth that we are made in God's image. Even if they do recognize its importance, they often see it as important only for their personal lives. But if one examines some of the key turning points in human history where we started treating whole groups of humans in more humane ways, one finds that the arguments for making change were undergirded by the reality that God made us in his image.

2. Theodoret of Cyrus, "Ecclesiastical History," 205.
3. Theodoret of Cyrus, "Ecclesiastical History," 205.
4. Theodoret of Cyrus, "Ecclesiastical History," 205.
5. Theodoret of Cyrus, "Ecclesiastical History," 205.

Unless you understand and learn this history, you will not recognize the transformations that have come about from humanity learning what it means that everyone is made in God's image. Unfortunately, this understanding and the transformation started haltingly and took hundreds, if not thousands, of years. But as we shall see, the results have been nothing short of a God-inspired recovery of his intentions for humanity.

CHAPTER FIVE

The Image of God and Humanizing the Marginalized

The Christian Roman Emperor Theodosius did not always act out his belief that all humans are made in the image of God. Theodoret of Cyprus shared another story about Theodosius that bears more similarities to the story from chapter 3 about the pagan emperor Caesar. Theodoret related how a revolt occurred in Thessalonica (ca. AD 390) in which a crowd beat and stoned some magistrates. In this case, Theodosius did not control his anger:

> The emperor was fired with anger when he heard the news, and unable to endure the rush of his passion, did not even check its onset by the curb of reason, but allowed his rage to be the minister of his vengeance. When the imperial passion had received its authority, as though itself an independent prince, it broke the bonds and yoke of reason, unsheathed swords of injustice right and left without distinction, and slew innocent and guilty together. No trial preceded the sentence. No condemnation was passed on the perpetrators of the crimes. Multitudes were mowed down like ears of corn in harvest-tide. It is said that seven thousand perished.[1]

1. Theodoret of Cyrus, "The Ecclesiastical History," trans. Blomfield Jackson, in *Nicene and Post-Nicene Fathers*, 2nd series, vol. 3, ed. Philip Schaff and Henry Wace (Christian Literature, 1892), 143.

The Christian bishop Ambrose eventually confronted Theodosius about the massacre and required him to submit to eight months of repentance and church discipline during which he could not take Communion or enter a church.

As Theodoret's story reminds us, throughout history humans have been incredibly adept at finding ways to dehumanize, mistreat, and murder other humans based on their tribe, race, ethnicity, sex, mental or physical abilities, health, age, gender, political beliefs, religious beliefs, civic actions, or a variety of other attributes. The bulk of our history provides examples of this fallen dehumanization.

However, there is another part of the story, one that has unfortunately been only a minor strand until the past two centuries. But its influence has grown and made an incredible impact on human history. It recognizes, like Macedonius, that we cannot reduce others according to their citizenship, race, ethnicity, gender, tribe, health, disabilities, or even their individual story. All of us, including emperors, must treat humans as image bearers of God. As this chapter will demonstrate, this growing understanding has brought about major social transformations.

Unfortunately, the enriching, dignity-providing power of understanding everyone as being made in God's image did not take hold quickly. Still, as humans grew to understand the doctrine that we are made in God's image, they drew on it to transform how we view the poor, the enslaved, women, and Native Americans. In this chapter, I provide a short historical summary of how the belief that humans are made in the image of God informed these vitally important developments during the first 1,550 years of the church's history.

Caring for Those Who Are Poor, Weak, and Disabled

One way that Christians changed ancient humanity's outlook regarding the marginalized concerned those who were poor or had broken or neglected bodies. Although today we take for granted that it is good to show generosity to the poor and care for those who are disabled, this moral presumption was not always with us. As one scholar, Kyle Harper, found of Rome, "The 'poor' simply did not exist as a social category within the machinery of ancient gift giving, and charity per se was not an articulate motivation for the distribution of beneficence."[2] In fact, Nadya Williams observed that in the ancient world, plenty of writers wrote self-help books about numerous topics, but "there is one topic on which no pagan writer ever wrote a how-to treatise: caring for others."[3]

Into this world, Christians brought the view that all humans are made in God's image and that God took on humanity in Christ, a truth that magnified the intrinsic worth of all humans. Both doctrines, the *imago Dei* and the incarnation, spurred the preservation and promotion of flourishing for all humans, including children, women, orphans, widows, the sick, the poor, and the disabled.

One finds this teaching in early church fathers such as Origen (ca. AD 185–254). When commenting on the story of Jesus conversing with the woman at the well, he observed, "For even the disciples marvel when they come, because they have already contemplated the magnitude of the divinity in him, marveling that such a great person would speak with a woman. But we, under the impulse of boasting and disdain, scorn those who are inferior, forgetting that 'let us make man according to our image, and according to our likeness' (Gen. 1:26) applies to each human being."[4]

One of the earliest documents where one finds this outlook applied is the Didache, which means "teaching." An early Christian teaching manual, considered to have been written late in the first century, it describes those who follow the way of darkness:

> There are they who persecute the good—lovers of a lie, not knowing the reward of righteousness, not cleaving to the good nor to righteous judgment, watching not for the good but for the bad, from whom meekness and patience are afar off, loving things that are vain, following after recompense, having no compassion on the needy, nor labouring for him that is in trouble, not knowing him that made them, murderers of children,

2. Kyle Harper, "Christianity and the Roots of Human Dignity in Late Antiquity," in *Christianity and Freedom: Historical Perspectives*, ed. Timothy Samuel Shah and Allen D. Hertzke (Cambridge University Press, 2016), 1:140.

3. Nadya Williams, *Mothers, Children, and the Body Politic: Ancient Christianity and the Recovery of Human Dignity* (IVP Academic, 2024), 153.

4. See Origen's "Commentary on John" in Joseph W. Trigg, *Origen* (Routledge, 1998), 174.

> *corrupters of the image of God*, who turn away from him that is in need, who oppress him that is in trouble, unjust judges of the poor, erring in all things. From all these, children, may ye be delivered.[5]

We see here the early Christian connection between corrupting the image of God and lacking concern for those who are poor, oppressed, and marginalized.

This attention would be expanded by various church fathers over the next three centuries in works such as Cyprian's essay *On Works and Alms* (ca. AD 251–257) and Ambrose's *Concerning Widows* (ca. AD 377). In the same period, Gregory of Nazianzus (AD 329–390) appealed to Christians to consider the suffering of the poor, since they are "our brothers in God, whether you like it or no; whose share in nature is the same as ours; who are formed of the same clay from the time of our first creation . . . more importantly, who have the same portion of the image of God just as we do and who keep it perhaps better, wasted though their bodies may be."[6] Marginalized humans, as fellow image bearers of God, now received special attention from Christians—attention we now often take for granted.

The Earliest Known Argument Against Slavery

As the stories of Joseph in Genesis and the Israelites in Egypt illustrate, slavery has existed since the earliest history of humanity. The emergence of the Greek and Roman Empires and the philosophies that developed within them did nothing to change that reality. As one scholar of these ancient societies observed, "Few societies have been so squarely constructed on the institution of slavery as were ancient Greece and Rome."[7] The institution had strong philosophical backing. As is well known, Aristotle claimed in his *Politics*, "It is clear that there are certain people who are free and certain people who are slaves [by nature], and it is both to their advantage, and just, for them to be slaves," a lie that

5. *Didache or Teaching of the Twelve Apostles*, trans. Charles H. Hoole (David Nutt, 1894), 79, emphasis added.

6. As quoted in Harper, "Christianity and the Roots of Human Dignity," 1:141.

7. Harper, "Christianity and the Roots of Human Dignity," 1:131.

David Brion Davis noted "would help shape virtually all subsequent proslavery thought."[8]

What eventually challenged this entrenched system? We know of no pronouncements against slavery until an ancient Christian bishop, Gregory of Nyssa, made this astounding argument against slavery in AD 381 in his commentary on Ecclesiastes and Solomon's many slaves:

> So when someone turns the property of God into his own property and arrogates dominion in his own kind, so as think of himself the owner of men and women, what is he doing but overstepping his own nature through pride, regarding himself as something different from his subordinates. . . . How many obols [a Roman unit of currency] did you reckon the equivalent of the likeness of God? God said, "let us make man in our image, after our likeness" [Gen. 1:26]. If he is the likeness of God who rules the whole earth, and has been granted authority over everything on earth from God, who is his buyer, tell me? Who is his seller? To God alone belongs this power.[9]

Gregory insisted that one could not put a price on humans made in the image of God. They should not be bought and sold. He would go on to say that everything about humanity "manifests royal dignity" due to its "exact likeness to the beauty of the archetype."[10]

Gregory's argument was consistent with the claim later made by the African theologian Augustine of Hippo in his *City of God* a few decades later: "The prime cause, then, of slavery is sin, which brings man under the dominion of his fellow."[11] Unfortunately, it would take almost 1,500 years for these arguments to lead to the abolition of slavery in most countries around the world. Indeed, as we will see in chapter 7, the Christians

8. Both Aristotle's quote and the subsequent quote are from David Brion Davis, *In the Image of God: Religion, Moral Values, and Our Heritage of Slavery* (Yale University Press, 2001), 128. Davis used a translation of Aristotle from Thomas Wiedemann, *Greek and Roman Slavery* (Croom & Helm, 1988), 18–20.

9. Gregory of Nyssa, *In Ecclesiasten* 4.1, Gregory, Bishop of Nyssa, "Homilies on Ecclesiastes," trans. Stuart G. Hall and Rachel Moriarty, in *Gregory of Nyssa, Homilies on Ecclesiastes: An English Version with Supporting Studies*, ed. Stuart G. Hall (de Gruyter, 1993), 78, quoted in Garnsey, *Ideas of Slavery*, 81–82.

10. Quoted in Andrew Louth, ed., *Ancient Christian Commentary on Scripture*, Genesis:1–11, vol. 1 (IVP Academic, 2001), 34.

11. Augustine, *City of God*, trans. Marcus Dods (Hendrickson, 2018), 627.

at the forefront of changing our thinking about slavery, like Gregory, appealed to the biblical idea that we are all made in God's image.

This important concept was a key reason why slavery was abolished in Christian and not Muslim cultures. Two scholars writing in the *Stanford Encyclopedia of Philosophy* observe that "there is no conceptual equivalent of the Western philosophical concept of 'person' in Arabic and in classic Islamic philosophy."[12] One reason for this omission is that Islam does not celebrate individuals as made in God's image. The authors go on to observe that the term *person* is largely Christian in origin.[13]

The Christian West's Celebration of the Individual Person and Human Responsibility

As mentioned in the last chapter, Christ and the apostles laid the groundwork for the view that humans are more than their social roles. We are not simply members of a tribe, our gender, our social class, and so on. Larry Siedentop shared in *Inventing the Individual*, "God's grace, revealed by the Christ, provided the means of entry into a truer self offered to all equally."[14] From this basis, Augustine developed a line of thought regarding the individual will that would honor our image-bearing capacities. Siedentop noted,

> For it is only a slight exaggeration to say that Augustine, drawing on Paul, invented the idea of the will. Arguably, the Christian assumption of moral equality made such an idea indispensable. It distanced individuals from whatever social roles they might occupy. As we have seen, the individual became the "primary" role, while other social roles became secondary. Such roles became the attributes of a subject endowed with a will. But they could not exhaust the subject's identity. Thus, individual identity was deemed to be extrinsic to social relations and the rightful

12. Thomas D. Williams and Jan Olof Bengtsson, "Personalism," in *The Stanford Encyclopedia of Philosophy*, ed. Edward N. Zalta (Summer 2022), https://plato.stanford.edu/archives/sum2022/entries/personalism/.

13. Williams and Bengtsson, "Personalism."

14. Larry Siedentop, *Inventing the Individual: The Origins of Western Liberalism* (Belknap, 2014), 303.

> criterion of them. The will acquired a privileged status as the threshold of divinity.[15]

Every individual, and not simply Roman citizens, Jews, men, or Pharisees, could now reclaim their original royal inheritance from God as humans with unique agency.

The radical nature of this change can be shown through the invention of a new genre of literature. Augustine wrote what is considered the first autobiography in history, his *Confessions*.[16] It is important to recognize that this book is not a tell-all intended for other humans like modern autobiographies; rather, as the title reveals, it is an individual confession to God. For Augustine, Christianity affirms that the individual matters before God, such that God desires an individual relationship and our confessions. Moreover, all humans have equal standing before God in that all are sinful and need his grace for salvation. Augustine's message, derived from the Bible and applied to individuals, sets forth the foundations for later arguments against both natural slavery and social hierarchy (e.g., the caste system). This outlook would also be combined with another biblical view supported by Augustine—that all humans are descended from one human family—to affirm both the equal dignity of all humans and their individuality.[17]

This emerging idea of the individual worth of every human would have significant ramifications in other ways. It universalized human responsibility in the way that God originally intended. Scholars have often pondered the question of why the rule of law took hold primarily in the Christian West. Two scholars, Avner Greif and Guido Tabellini, contend that one reason for the rise of the rule of law in the West pertains to the different identities used to establish moral obligations in the East and West.[18] If someone's loyalty group—and thus their scope of moral obligation—rests with their clan (as it did in Confucian China) or their

15. Siedentop, *Inventing the Individual*, 301.

16. Augustine, *Confessions*, trans. F. J. Sheed (Hackett, 2006). For a discussion of Augustine's *Confessions* as the first autobiography, see Kim Paffenroth and Kevin L. Hughes, eds., *Augustine and Liberal Education* (Ashgate, 2000).

17. Augustine, *City of God*, 118.

18. Avner Greif, Joel Mokyr, and Guido Tabellini, *Two Paths to Prosperity: Culture and Institutions in Europe and China, 1000 to 2000* (Princeton University Press, 2025). See also Avner Greif and Guido Tabellini, "The Clan and the Corporation: Sustaining

place in an empire (as it did in the Roman Empire), then a broad rule of law outside the clan or empire, as well as organization building beyond the clan or empire, becomes much more difficult.

In contrast to the East, Western Christians established a more generalized morality not based on an identity related to a clan or even the empire but rather on the claim that all humans are made in the image of God and are ultimately responsible to him. These differences then applied to moral obligations such as honor, contract keeping, charity, and a variety of other responsibilities. Christians then expected those outside their clans both to know general moral obligations and to keep them based on one's identity as humans made in God's image. In other words, the identity you use to determine your moral obligations makes a tremendous difference in the scope of your moral obligations and how you view others with different sub-identities. For those who believe that we are made in God's image, the concept of universal human moral responsibility before God becomes possible.

Women: A Mixed Influence

The church fathers also upheld the dignity of women by affirming that they, too, are made in God's image. Church fathers such as Clement of Alexandria (AD 150–215), Athanasius (ca. 296–373), Gregory of Nyssa (ca. 335–394), John Chrysostom (347–407), Augustine (354–430), and Cyril of Alexandria (ca. 376–444) all held that women were made in God's image.[19] For example, in Augustine's commentary on Genesis he wrote, "A woman, for all her physical qualities as a woman, is actually renewed in the spirit of her mind in the knowledge of God according to the image of her Creator, and therein there is no male or female. . . . By

Cooperation in China and Europe," *Journal of Comparative Economics* 45, no. 1 (2017): 1–35.

19. Walter J. Burghardt, *The Image of God in Man, According to Cyril of Alexandria* (Catholic University of America Press, 1957); Gregory of Nyssa, *On the Human Image of God*, ed. and trans. John Behr (Oxford University Press, 2023), 100; Augustine, *The Literal Meaning of Genesis*, in *Ancient Christian Writers*, trans. John Hammond Taylor (Paulist Press, 1982), 99. For John Chrysostom's commentary from the fifth century, see "Genesis 1:26," Catena Bible, accessed November 8, 2025, https://catenabible.com/com/5838d595205c248f42e5185d.

the same token, in the original creation of man, inasmuch as woman was a human being, she certainly had a mind, and a rational mind, and therefore she also was made to the image of God."[20] This understanding of women as made in God's image established the foundation for later Christian thinkers to affirm this point.

That being said, some of these early church fathers still held to beliefs about women they had inherited from the wider Greek and Roman culture that led them to qualify what this meant. Cyril of Alexandria did not view women as equal to men in many spheres of life such as their ability to reason, learn, and acquire virtue.[21] Augustine took a different approach that denigrated female bodies instead of their reasoning. Augustine's initial comment, "for all her physical qualities as a woman," showed that his view that women are made in God's image did not extend to them as embodied creatures.[22]

One scholar, E. Ann Matter, describes how the distinction played out for the next thousand years among Christian thinkers: "Women are equal to men (and therefore in the image of God) according to our humanity but NOT according to our female embodiment."[23] Unfortunately, Augustine's theology was influenced by his past dalliance with Gnostic ideas and his earlier difficulties with lust for and sexual immorality with women. It was not until the Reformation in the sixteenth century that Christian scholars affirmed that women, like men, are created in God's image, including in their physical bodies.

The Humanity and Treatment of Native Americans

In 1510, a Dominican priest, Antonio de Montesinos, arrived with fellow members of his order in what today is the Dominican Republic. Upon arrival, a mere eighteen years after Columbus's arrival in 1492, he and his fellow Dominicans were shocked at what they saw. The

20. Augustine, *Literal Meaning of Genesis*, 99.

21. Burghardt, *Image of God in Man*, 126–40.

22. E. Ann Matter, "The Undebated Debate: Gender and the Image of God in Medieval Theology," in *Gender in Debate from the Early Middle Ages to the Renaissance*, ed. Thelma S. Fenster and Clare A. Lees (Palgrave, 2002), 41–56.

23. Matter, "Undebated Debate," 41.

Spanish had gone about conquering and enslaving the native people most horrifically. Whipping, rape, and mutilation of the population were commonplace. So, too, were periodic massive injustices. In the conquering of Cuba a few years later, the Spaniards simply massacred a whole village of 2,500 natives, including women and children, without provocation.[24]

By December of 1511, the Dominicans had seen enough. They all agreed that the evil treatment of the native population needed to be addressed. They also agreed that the Dominican friar Antonio de Montesinos would present a sermon signed by all of them that would address the evils they saw. According to our record of the sermon, he declared, "I am the voice of one crying out in the wilderness," and would go on to preach, "you are all in mortal sin, that you live in it and will die in it, because of the cruelty and oppression with which you treat these innocent people. . . . Are they not men? Have they no soul? No reason? Are you not required to love them as you love yourselves?"[25]

The sermon enraged the Spanish settlers, who saw their economic interest attacked, and they later went to ask Montesinos to retract the sermon. He refused. Instead, the Dominican friars said in the following sermon that anyone who continued in the ill-treatment of the natives would be refused Communion. The courage of these Dominicans, who saw the native population as image bearers of God, would have reverberations throughout history.

Columbus Day / Indigenous Peoples Day should serve as a reminder to all Christians of the inhumane treatment of Native Americans by certain groups of Europeans. Moreover, what is even more problematic is that some Christian scholars in the universities and churches of Europe used their power and intellectual abilities to justify the enslavement of Native Americans. But this day should also remind us not only of these courageous Dominican friars in Hispaniola but also a noble band of Christian scholars who thought differently, reasoned counterculturally using the truth that all humans are made in God's image, and remained

24. Bartolomé de las Casas, *Witness: Writings of Bartolomé de las Casas*, ed. George Sanderlin (Orbis Books, 1971), 51.

25. Bartolomé de las Casas, "A Voice in the Wilderness: Brother Antonio Montesino," in *The Dominican Republic Reader*, ed. Eric Paul Roorda, Lauren Derby, and Raymundo González (Duke University Press, 2014), 53–54.

faithful to the liberating message of the gospel in a way that did not serve the material interests of their rulers.

The source of this conflict came from a question that emerged from the European "discovery" of the Americas: How should political representatives of Christian countries treat the First Nations population? Two problematic streams of thought emerged and combined to produce dreadful results. A third stream, however, set forth abundant life that depended on the theological truth that we are made in God's image.

The Problem with Christian Aristotelians

Some university and church leaders, in determining how to treat the First Nations population, turned to a respected pagan from antiquity instead of the Bible. Lewis Hawke noted in his *Aristotle and the American Indians*, "Aristotle's authority remained so strong among Christian thinkers that some eminent Spaniards did not hesitate to apply his doctrine of natural slavery to the Indians."[26] Scholars point to a 1510 writing by John Major (Mair), a Scottish theologian who taught at the University of Paris, as the first instance of applying Aristotle's understanding of natural slavery to Native Americans, or "barbarians" as those who made this application called them.[27]

Major's approach then was copied by numerous Spanish thinkers in various debates before the Spanish Crown, particularly by the theologian Juan Ginés de Sepúlveda, who would defend the actions of the Spanish conquistadors. These scholars failed to recognize that pagan authorities must be interrogated and rejected if their view of humanity operates outside the Christian understanding. Instead, they allowed Aristotle to trump Scripture.

26. Lewis Hawke, *Aristotle and the American Indians: A Study in Race Prejudice in the Modern World* (Henry Regnery, 1959), 1.

27. Roger Ruston, *Human Rights and the Image of God* (SCM, 2004), 73; Hawke, *Aristotle and the American Indians*, 16; Bartolomé de las Casas, *Bartolomé de Las Casas and the Defense of Amerindian Rights: A Brief History with Documents*, ed. Lawrence A. Clayton and David M. Lantigua (University of Alabama Press, 2020), 87. John Mair was not alone. Numerous other Christian thinkers affirmed this view. See, for example, the English scholar John Case, who wrote a commentary on Aristotle's *Politics* in which he heartily defended Aristotle's views on natural slavery. See "Book 1," accessed November 9, 2025, https://philological.cal.bham.ac.uk/sphaera/1eng.html.

The Problem with OT Israel-Typology Christian Thinking

A second group of Christians was more faithful to Scripture. Yet they still held a deeply flawed way of thinking about the relationship with Native American tribes as political groups within the Christian narrative. These were the early settlers, both Spanish and English, who saw themselves as Israel entering the promised land filled with Canaanites. Thus, they perceived that they could justify taking the land, conquering the people, and even enslaving or murdering them by copying Israel's holy war approach.

For instance, the Spanish lawyer Juan López de Palacios Rubios famously led the Council of Castile that published the 1510 *Requerimiento*, a document to be read to Native American communities the Spaniards encountered. It proclaimed, "Of all these nations God our Lord gave charge to one man, called St. Peter, that he should be Lord and Superior of all the men in the world, that all should obey him, and that he should be the head of the whole human race, wherever men should live, and under whatever law, sect, or belief they should be; and he gave him the world for his kingdom and jurisdiction." It then declared, in a manner reminiscent of Deuteronomy 28–30, the consequences of the Native Americans' choice to obey or defy:

> If you do so, you will do well, and that which you are obliged to do to their Highnesses, and we in their name shall receive you in all love and charity, and shall leave you, your wives, and your children, and your lands, free without servitude, . . . But, if you do not do this, and maliciously make delay in it, I certify to you that, with the help of God, we shall powerfully enter into your country, and shall make war against you in all ways and manners that we can, and shall subject you to the yoke and obedience of the Church and of their Highnesses; we shall take you and your wives and your children, and shall make slaves of them, and as such shall sell and dispose of them as their Highnesses may command.[28]

28. "Requerimiento, 1510," National Humanities Center, accessed November 9, 2025, https://nationalhumanitiescenter.org/pds/amerbegin/contact/text7/requirement.pdf. For the original Spanish version, see Francisco Morales Padrón, *Teoría y leyes de la conquista* (Ediciones Cultura Hispánica del Centro Iberoamericano de Cooperación, 1979), 331–37.

Unfortunately, a consistent mistake among Christians who long for more political power is envisioning themselves as ancient Israel entering the promised land—a hermeneutical error that has been employed throughout history.

The good news is that other influential Christian practitioners and professors produced a better way of thinking about Native Americans.

Countering the Two Medieval Mistakes: Remembering the Image of God

The scholar Francisco de Vitoria (ca. 1483–1546) was the first thinker to set forth a theologically informed approach to non-Christian peoples that relied on the key theological doctrine that all humans are made in God's image. By 1537, when he published his work on this subject, the Dominican Vitoria had heard the reports from his colleagues mentioned earlier. He not only affirmed their original condemnation of the Spanish conquistadors' behavior but also established the argument against mistreatment on extended theological grounds.

Vitoria argued that Native Americans should be understood as being made in God's image and therefore sharing in God's mandate to exercise dominion over his creation. He acknowledged that a few previous Christian thinkers held that one lost the image through sin (contra Gen. 9:6), but Vitoria rightfully dismissed this view as a "lunatic heresy."[29] He pointed out that this view is inconsistent with Scripture and with church fathers such as Augustine, "for man is the image of God by his inborn nature, that is by his rational powers. Hence he cannot lose his dominion by mortal sin."[30] Thus, he argued that Native Americans shared full humanity and the ability to exercise the dominion specified in Genesis 1. Overall, Vitoria's claim that Native Americans were made in God's image was the fundamental premise of his argument.[31]

29. Francisco de Vitoria, *Political Writings*, ed. Anthony Pagden and Jeremy Lawrence (Cambridge University Press, 1991), 243.

30. Vitoria, *Political Writings*, 242.

31. William Bain, "Vitoria: The Law of War, Saving the Innocent, and the Image of God," *Just and Unjust Military Intervention*, ed. Stefano Recchia and Jennifer M. Welsh (Cambridge University Press, 2013), 71, https://doi.org/10.1017/CBO9781107323681.004.

The Christian witness of these Dominicans had a profound influence on Bartolomé de las Casas (1484–1566). He immigrated to Hispaniola (present-day Haiti and the Dominican Republic) when he was a layperson. As one of the first settlers, he also benefited from Native American slave labor. However, de las Casas would later repent of his use of Native American slave labor and become a Dominican friar himself. He would go on to be the most famous early voice speaking out against the cruel treatment of Native Americans.

His most well-known writing is *A Brief Account of the Destruction of the Indies*. In this 1542 work outlining the cruelties of Spanish colonialists to Native Americans, he made this argument: "We read of old, of the Ten Persecutions wherein the Primitive Christians were destroyed by the Cruelties of the Heathen Emperours: but now read of Christians, the Professors of a Religion grounded upon Love and Charity, massacring, where there was no cause of Antipathy, but their own obstinate Barbarism; as if because their Wickedness had so far transform'd them into Devils, they were resolved to deface the image of God, so innocently conversing among them."[32] As can be seen, he specifically built his case against the cruel treatment of Native Americans on the fact that they are "born and raised up in the image of God."[33]

Later, he tells of this horrible story: "In some province of new Spain, it happened that a Spaniard being a hunting, his dogs seemed to him to be a hungry, whereupon he took a little infant out of the mother's arms, and cutting off the thighs and arm of the child, cast it to his dogs, and when they had devoured those, he cast the whole body to them. Thus, we see how [the Spanish conquistadors] were delivered over to a reprobate sense; and what a value they put upon these creatures formed after the Image of God."[34] Again, de las Casas drove home the point that Native Americans should be treated as the image bearers of God that they are.

32. Bartolomé de las Casas, *An Account, Much Abbreviated, of the Destruction of the Indies with Related Texts*, ed. Franklin Knight, trans. Andrew Hurley (Hackett, 2003), 16–17.

33. Lawrence A. Clayton and David M. Lantigua, *Bartolomé de Las Casas and the Defense of Amerindian Rights: A Brief History with Documents* (University of Alabama Press, 2020), 8.

34. Bartolomé de las Casas, *Account*, 64.

Bartolomé de las Casas later defended the humanity of Native Americans in front of the Spanish Crown in 1550 against the famous Catholic theologian Juan Ginés de Sepúlveda. In that debate, he explicitly rejected the claim that Native Americans should be considered natural servants, a view derived from Aristotle, whom de las Casas described as "a pagan now burning in Hell, whose principles should be accepted insofar as they conform to our Christian religion."[35] In contrast, de las Casas declared in another argument,

> If we want to be sons of Christ and followers of the truth of the gospel, we should consider that, even though these peoples may be completely barbaric, they are nevertheless created in God's image. They are not forsaken by divine providence that they are incapable of attaining Christ's kingdom. They are our brothers, redeemed by Christ's most precious blood, no less than the wisest and most learned men in the whole world. Finally, we must consider it possible that some of them are predestined to become renowned and glorious in Christ's kingdom.[36]

He then appealed directly to Scripture:

> According to Paul: "I owe a duty to Greeks just as much as to barbarians, to the educated just [as] much as to the uneducated, and it is this that makes me want to bring the Good News to you too in Rome [Rom. 1:14–15]." Christ wanted love to be called his single commandment. This we owe to all men. Nobody is exempted. "There is no room for distinction between Greek and Jew, between the circumcised and the uncircumcised, or between barbarian and Scythian, slave and free man. There is only Christ: he is everything and is in everything [Col. 3:17]."[37]

35. As quoted in Lewis Hanke, *All Mankind Is One: A Study of the Disputation Between Bartolomé de Las Casas and Juan Ginés de Sepúlveda in 1550 on the Intellectual and Religious Capacity of the American Indians* (Northern Illinois University Press, 1974), 11. For the full source, see Clayton and Lantigua, *Defense of Amerindian Rights*. For more on this topic, see David M. Lantigua, "The Image of God, Christian Rights Talk, and the School of Salamanca," *Journal of Law and Religion* 31, no. 1 (February 2016): 19–41.

36. Clayton and Lantigua, *Defense of Amerindian Rights*, 89.

37. Clayton and Lantigua, *Defense of Amerindian Rights*, 89.

To end this point, he concluded, "Good-bye, Aristotle! From Christ, the eternal truth, we have the command 'You must love your neighbor as yourself [Matt. 22:39].'"[38]

As a result of his courageous witness, the Spanish Crown attempted to put an end to the murder, enslavement, and overall dehumanization of Native American peoples. Unfortunately, we must always remember that good theological thinking is never enough. It must then be transferred into legal structures and actions. As Brian Tierney noted, "In the end, all the writings on behalf of the Indians did little or nothing to ameliorate their plight. The battles that were sometimes won in the debating halls of Salamanca and Madrid were nearly always lost among the hard realities of life in Mexico or Peru."[39] Good theology, good laws, and good people did not always hold sway with evil conquistadors.

The good news for us today, however, is that we can learn and apply these important historical lessons to our own lives and institutions. The end of this book explores this application. Before getting to those lessons, however, I will outline in chapters 6 and 7 how an understanding of the image of God transformed education and helped bring down slavery.

38. Clayton and Lantigua, *Defense of Amerindian Rights*, 89.

39. Brian Tierney, *The Idea of Natural Rights: Studies on Natural Rights, Natural Law, and Church Law, 1150–1625* (Scholars Press, 1997), 256.

CHAPTER SIX

The Image of God and the Transformation of Education

> As Man was at first made in the moral Image or Likeness to God, so the recovery of that Image is the greatest duty and highest perfection.
>
> —Yale College President Thomas Clap, 1765[1]

Education is supposed to change you. It is supposed to move you closer to some higher ideal or end. But what is that ideal or end? I have asked hundreds of college students around the nation, "What is the purpose of higher education?"

The answers I receive are not surprising, but they are disappointing. Students tend to have an extremely narrow and self-serving understanding of the university's purpose. Ninety-two percent of students give self-oriented answers to the question. They view the university as a place to "find a career," "make connections," "get more money in life," "get a degree," or "have fun."

Only 8 percent of students mention an other- or God-oriented purpose. These students want to "cultivate skills that you can use in the real

1. Thomas Clap, *An Essay on the Nature and Foundation of Moral Virtue and Obligation: Being a Short Introduction to the Study of Ethics: For the Use of the Students of Yale-College* (B. Mecom, 1765), 54.

world to better the community," "use your knowledge to help others," and "develop a skill set and a toolbox with which I can glorify God." Still, even these students do not articulate an understanding of higher education's purpose related to what some important early Christian designers of the university had in mind. These thinkers articulated the university's purpose by building on the core truth that we are made to be and to bear God's image.

The Christian Origins and Purpose of the University

Christians invented the university in the late twelfth and early thirteenth centuries.[2] What did early leaders consider the purpose of the university? It started with the important truth that we are all made in God's image. For example, scholars consider Hugh of St. Victor (1096–1141) an architect of one of the early Parisian cathedral schools that would be a blueprint for the University of Paris (considered one of the first universities).[3] His book describing the purpose of higher education conceived it as much more than a self-oriented project, like most students do today. Instead, he placed the purpose of higher education within the overall Christian story.

He recognized that although we are all made in God's image, the fall marred this image. The good news is that Christ has provided a way for us to be reconciled with God and to fulfill his purpose. Thus, we must recognize that more fully becoming an image bearer of God, like a seed that can grow into a fruit tree, requires a sanctified form of Christian education to obtain the purpose God originally had for humanity as image bearers. Consequently, Hugh claimed regarding higher education's

2. See Jacques Verger, "Patterns," in *A History of the University in Europe*, vol. 1, *Universities in the Middle Ages*, ed. Hilde de Ridder-Symoens (Cambridge University Press, 1992), 35. Verger affirms, "It is no doubt true that other civilizations, prior to, or wholly alien to, the medieval West, such as the Roman Empire, Byzantium, Islam, or China, were familiar with forms of higher education which a number of historians, for the sake of convenience, have sometimes described as universities. Yet a closer look makes it plain that the institutional reality was altogether different and, no matter what has been said on the subject, there is no real link such as would justify us in associating them with medieval universities in the West" (35).

3. Perry L. Glanzer, Nathan F. Alleman, and Todd C. Ream, *Restoring the Soul of the University: Unifying Christian Higher Education in a Fragmented Age* (InterVarsity, 2017).

purpose, "This is our entire task—the restoration of our nature and the removal of our deficiency."[4] He maintained that teaching students the liberal arts was particularly meant to help "restore within us the divine likeness, a likeness which to us is a form but to God is his nature."[5] The restoration process Hugh envisioned was different than earlier pagan approaches to education.

Early Pagan Education

Greek and Roman society first created education in what has historically been called the liberal arts: those disciplines that are not merely professional skills, such as learning to be an excellent trader. Most American universities now provide this same type of education through what they call general education or a core curriculum. Yet, unlike today, these Greek and Roman thinkers envisioned this education as being only for free men with the leisure time to study. Women, slaves, and most working men were excluded from this education. The Roman thinker Seneca articulated this vision: "I respect no study and deem no study good, which results in money-making. . . . Hence you see why 'liberal studies' are so called; it is because they are studies worthy of a free-born gentleman."[6]

Moreover, the central purpose of this education was different than the Christian view not only because Hugh used a different overarching meta-narrative to guide its purpose but also because it entailed a different understanding of *aretē* or excellence (the word used for God's excellence and the excellences we are to acquire, mentioned in 2 Peter 1) and different methods by which to achieve it.

In the 2004 movie *Troy*, an early scene shows a young boy helping Achilles (played by Brad Pitt) get ready for battle with the champion from the Thessalonians, whom the boy describes as "the biggest man I've

4. Hugh of St. Victor, *The Didascalicon of Hugh of St. Victor: A Medieval Guide to the Arts*, trans. Jerome Taylor (Columbia University Press, 1991), 52.

5. Hugh of St. Victor, *De arca Noe morali iv.i* (PL, CLXXVI, 663B), quoted in Hugh of St. Victor, *Didascalicon*, 171n132.

6. Seneca, "On Liberal and Vocational Studies," in *The Great Tradition: Classic Readings on What It Means to Be an Educated Human Being*, ed. Richard M. Gamble (ISI Books, 2007), 98.

ever seen." The young boy goes on to confess, "I wouldn't want to fight him." Achilles responds, "That's why no one will remember your name."[7] In that brief exchange, we gain insight into the early understanding of *aretē* in heroic Greek society (eighth century BC). The ultimate virtues relate to courage and physical prowess by which one gains honor. Moreover, as Alasdair MacIntyre noted of this arrangement, "Honor is conferred by one's peers and without honor a man is without worth."[8] Lacking an understanding of all humans as made in God's image, they had no concept of intrinsic human worth. Death in this heroic age was a terrible evil, but it could be overcome, not by eternal life but by having the stories of one's courage live forever.

Later Greek thinkers in the fifth and fourth centuries BC expanded on and transformed this view of excellence in important ways that brought it closer to a Christian view. They still saw *aretē* as essential virtue, but they expanded the human understanding of excellence. For example, both Plato and Aristotle thought education should lead one to the truth and should form a person intellectually and morally to achieve the good or blessed life and the just society. The key excellences or virtues necessary in such a society were not only courage but also wisdom, temperance, and justice.

Still, the means they proposed were not sufficient for the task. Plato thought dialectical reasoning would be enough to develop virtuous people. Aristotle also emphasized that the formation of habits based on reasoning was necessary to achieve the virtues required for a good life. Neither one came close to a Christian understanding of humanity and our need for God to assist us in this formation.

Roman educators inherited this Greek concept. One finds this view expressed in the original *Gladiator* movie. In one scene, the Roman emperor, Marcus Aurelius, one of the authors of a famous book on Stoic philosophy, meets with his son, Commodus. Commodus confesses to his father, "You wrote to me once listing the four chief virtues—wisdom, justice, fortitude, and temperance. As I read the list, I knew that I had none of them."[9] Not surprisingly, he then goes on to kill his father.

7. *Troy*, directed by Wolfgang Petersen (Warner Home Video, 2004), DVD.

8. Alasdair MacIntyre, *After Virtue*, 2nd ed. (University of Notre Dame Press, 1984), 125.

9. *Gladiator*, directed by Ridley Scott (DreamWorks Distribution, 2000), DVD.

These cardinal virtues and the liberal arts, however, were not taught to all humans and social classes. Instead, the Romans emphasized that the virtues and an ideal liberal arts education had a key practical use: They helped one become an excellent orator who could persuade one's fellow Roman citizens.

Placing Education in the Christian Story

Placing the purpose of higher education in the Christian story, as Hugh did, however, transformed the purpose and substance of education. First, he made clear that neither heroic deeds nor virtues alone give us worth. That comes from being made in God's image. Second, Hugh wrote, "The more we are conformed to the Divine Nature, the more do we possess Wisdom, for then there begins to shine forth again in us what has forever existed in the divine Idea or Pattern, coming and going in us but standing changeless in God."[10] In other words, Hugh countered the Greek and Roman idea that the liberal arts are merely education for a select few free men who rule an empire. Instead, he affirmed that education is meant for all humans—everyone made in God's image—to help restore the divine image in which we are made.[11]

This kind of education serves to lead us to friendship with God and acquire his wisdom and justice. Hugh wrote regarding the role of education, "Now there are two things which restore the divine likeness in man, namely the contemplation of truth and the practice of virtue. For man resembles God in being wise and just—though, to be sure, man is but changeably so while God stands changelessly both wise and just."[12] For Hugh, Christian educators should assist with this majestic endeavor by fulfilling what Christ has already accomplished. Educators

10. Hugh of St. Victor, *De arca Noe morali* iv.i (PL, CLXXVI, 663B), quoted in Hugh of St. Victor, *Didascalicon*, 171n132.

11. Walter Rüegg claimed the idea that we are equal image bearers of God "found an institutional arrangement for scientific and scholarly study in the setting provided by the university." Walter Rüegg, "Themes," in *A History of the University in Europe*, vol. 1, *Universities in the Middle Ages*, ed. Hilde de Ridder-Symoens (Cambridge University Press, 1992), 32–33.

12. Hugh of St. Victor, *Didascalicon of Hugh of St. Victor*, 54–55.

are supposed to be God's instrument for helping rebuild his image in humanity through the liberal arts.

Moreover, he reminds both teachers and students that, unlike Greek or Roman educators, we must recognize the need for God's help with this task. He writes, "Since the counsel of man is weak and ineffective without divine aid, arouse yourself to prayer and ask the help of him without whom you can accomplish no good thing, so that by his grace, which going before you has enlightened you, he may guide your feet, as you follow, onto the road of peace; and so that he may bring that which as yet is in your will alone, to concrete effect in good performance. . . . God wishes to work with you; you are not forced, but you are helped."[13]

We see in Hugh's quote what the famous historian of universities, Walter Rüegg, observed was necessary for the development of the first universities—namely, the belief that humans are made in the image of God and, as a result, possess a particular kind of freedom to engage in creativity similar to God. Rüegg claimed, "Respect for the individual as a reflection of the macrocosm or as having been formed in the image of God laid the foundation for the gradually realized freedom of scientific and scholarly research and teaching."[14] As mentioned in chapter 3, the reality that we are made in God's image allows us to celebrate an appropriate form of human freedom and creativity. That creativity and freedom nourished the foundation of the first universities.

The Unfortunate Undermining

Unfortunately, these revolutionary Christian truths received limited acceptance among European Christian universities. One major hindrance was the incorporation of Aristotelian metaphysics and moral philosophy into the liberal arts curriculum of the first universities. Aristotle's hierarchical understanding of human society that accepted slavery and other social and educational inequities as natural superseded the more egalitarian Jewish and Christian view.

13. Hugh of St. Victor, *Didascalicon of Hugh of St. Victor*, 132.
14. Rüegg, "Themes," 32–33.

Aristotle's *Nicomachean Ethics* and *Politics* ultimately became the primary course texts used in the moral philosophy classes of Christian medieval European universities for the next 350 years.[15] The universities taught these Aristotelian ideas in the liberal arts course on moral philosophy.[16] Thus, "undergraduate" students educated only in the liberal arts were not always encouraged to build their understanding of humanity's core moral function on the concept of the *imago Dei* but rather on Aristotle's elitist and hierarchical understanding of humanity.

The incorporation of pagan falsehoods into our ethics, the university, and society had profound ramifications. One result is that it would take even longer for the key idea that we are *all* persons made in God's image to replace Aristotelian ideas used to justify the dehumanization of Muslims, Native Americans, Africans, and women—a point revealed in the last chapter.

A second problematic belief that sprang up among some scholars during the Middle Ages was the belief that humans lost the image of God after the fall.[17] According to this view, only Christians could then recover the image of God and exercise the responsibilities that God entrusted to humanity in creation. As one can imagine, such a view has a tremendous influence on the degree to which non-Christians can be involved in engaging in dominion over creation and human society. Thus, it would take a new group of Christian thinkers to correct these problematic

15. Laurence Brockliss, "Curricula," in *A History of the University in Europe*, vol. 2, *Universities in Early Modern Europe, 1500–1800*, ed. Hilde De Ridder-Symoens (Cambridge University Press, 1996).

16. Gordon Leff, "The *Trivium* and the Three Philosophies," in *A History of the University in Europe*, vol. 1, *Universities in the Middle Ages*, ed. Walter Rüegg (Cambridge University Press, 1992), 307–36.

17. Two scholastic scholars who held this view were John Wycliffe and Richard FitzRalph. Anthony Pagden and J. Lawrence note, "Their account accepts that man is made in the likeness of God; however, they also argue that this likeness and the dominion consequent to it are corrupted by sin, the conclusion being: 'the image of God is not in the sinner, hence the sinner cannot have such dominion [what I label stewardship].'" Francisco de Vitoria, "On the American Indians," in *Political Writings*, ed. Anthony Pagden and J. Lawrence (Cambridge University Press, 1991), 84. One such Puritan was John Owen. See Suzanne McDonald, "Historical and Theological Studies: The Pneumatology of the Lost Image in John Owen," *Westminster Theological Journal* 71, no. 2 (2009): 323–35.

errors. Some of those thinkers were university-educated Christians such as Bartolomé de las Casas, who fought for the biblical view of how to treat Native Americans. Others, however, were teachers.

One of the influential figures who helped spread this idea was Pierre de la Ramée (1515–1572), commonly known as Peter Ramus, a professor at the University of Paris. In contrast to John Major, the University of Paris professor mentioned in the last chapter who used Aristotle's teaching to claim that Native Americans are natural slaves, Ramus took a highly critical view of Aristotle.

For the decade before his death, Ramus criticized the extensive use of Aristotle in the teaching of ethics. It was through Aristotle, he complained,

> where the boy learns a mass of impieties: for example, that the principle and ideals of "the good" are innate in every man, that all the virtues are within his own power, that he acquires them by means of nature, art, and labor, and that for this work, so grand and so sublime, man has need of neither the aid nor the cooperation of God. Nothing about providence; not a word about divine justice; in short, since, in the eyes of Aristotle, souls are mortal, the happiness of man is reduced to this perishable life. . . . Such is the philosophy out of which we build the foundation of our religion![18]

Overall, he wanted Christian theology and ethics to replace Aristotelian metaphysics and moral philosophy as foundational courses within the liberal arts curriculum.

Most importantly, Ramus emphasized that the basis for this replacement stands on the doctrine that we are all made in the image of God. Due to the fall, we need to restore the defaced image. He wrote, "For man (I keep repeating this) is created in the image of God, and he is ordered to restore it whenever he falls away from it by sin: Col. 3. You have put on the new nature, which is being renewed in knowledge after the image

18. Frank Pierrepont Graves, *Peter Ramus and the Educational Reformation of the Sixteenth Century* (Macmillan, 1912), 174–75. For the original Latin, see Peter Ramus, *Petri Rami Pro philosophica parisiensis academiae disciplina oratio* (Paris, 1557), https://books.google.com/books?id=rFFV082xNp0C.

of its Creator."[19] This rebuke of the supposedly Christian university's slavish adherence to Aristotelianism would take root in other countries such as England, the Netherlands, Scotland, and the American colonies, where Reformed thinking that followed after Ramus was embraced.[20]

One of the fascinating early multivolume English works that discusses what it means for humans to be made in God's image was written by the Reformed Scottish minister John Weemes (also sometimes Wemyss, ca. 1579–1636). In his book *The Portraiture of the Image of God in Man* (1632), like Ramus, he too faults Greek thinkers for thinking they can attain the good life without the aid of God's virtues.[21] He also sets forth the two-part purpose noted earlier. First, that humans restore the marred image of God by both stewardship over his creation and acquiring his virtues. Interestingly, Weemes would also be one of the first Christians to speak against the expulsion of Jews from Christian countries and one of the first writers to point out that people with different skin colors are all made in God's image (a subject covered in the next chapter).

Universal Education for Everyone, Including Women and the Poor

One of Ramus's students would go on to instruct another famous educational reformer, John Amos Comenius (1592–1670). Comenius is famous for being an early proponent of universal education for all people, including women and the poor.[22] The basis of his argument in *The Great*

19. As quoted in Peter Sharrat, "Peter Ramus and Imitation: Image, Sign and Sacrament," in *Image and Symbol in the Renaissance*, Yale French Studies 47 (Yale University Press, 1972), 28.

20. Perry L. Glanzer, Nathan F. Alleman, and Todd C. Ream, *Restoring the Soul of the University: Unifying Christian Higher Education in a Fragmented Age* (InterVarsity, 2017).

21. John Weemes, *The Portraiture of the Image of God in Man* (London, 1632), 152–58, https://archive.org/details/portma00weem/page/n3/mode/2up.

22. The early Protestant Reformers were strong advocates of education for everyone, including boys and girls. Martin Luther famously argued for compulsory education for both young boys and girls, arguing, "Would to God each town had also a girls' school, in which girls might be taught the Gospel for an hour daily, either in German or Latin!" Martin Luther, "An Open Letter to the Christian Nobility of the German Nation Concerning the Reform of the Christian Estate," in *Works of*

Didactic rested on recovering the implications of the doctrine that we are all made in God's image:

> The following reasons will establish that not the children of the rich or the powerful only, but of all alike, boys and girls, both noble and ignoble, rich and poor, in all cities and towns, villages and hamlets, should be sent to school. In the first place, all who have been born . . . have been born with the same end in view, namely that they be . . . rational creatures, the lords of other creatures, and *the images of their Creator*. . . . God Himself has frequently asserted that with Him there is no respect of persons . . . so that, if, while we admit some to the culture of the intellect, we exclude others, we commit an injury not only against those who share the same nature as ourselves, but against God Himself.[23]

For Comenius, the idea that every human has dignity, a result of being made in God's image, has profound educational implications—namely, that educators should seek "for the full power of development into full humanity not of one particular person or a few or even many, but of every single individual, young and old, rich and poor, noble and ignoble, men and women—in a word, of every human born on earth, with the ultimate aim of providing education to the entire human race regardless of age, class, sex and nationality."[24] In other words, everyone is made in the image of God, meaning all humans need education for development.

Understanding that all humans are made in God's image led Comenius to the conclusion that there was no reason why women should be kept from education. He reasoned this way:

> They [women] also are formed in the image of God, and share in His grace and in the kingdom of the world to come. They are endowed with equal sharpness of mind and capacity for knowledge (often with more than the opposite sex), and they are able to attain the highest positions, since they have often been called by God Himself to rule over nations, to give

Martin Luther, trans. C. M. Jacobs (A. J. Holman, 1915), 50, https://www.onthewing.org/user/Luther%20-%20Nobility%20of%20the%20German%20Nation.pdf.

23. John Amos Comenius, *The Great Didactic*, ed. and trans. M. W. Keatinge (Adam and Charles Black, 1907), 66, emphasis added.

24. John Amos Comenius, *Comenius's Pampaedia or Universal Education*, trans. A. M. O. Dobbie (Buckland, 1986), 19.

> sound advice to kings and princes, to the study of medicine and of other things which benefit the human race, even to the office of prophesying and of inveighing against priests and bishops. Why, therefore, should we admit them to the alphabet, and afterwards drive them away from books?[25]

Comenius would go on to become one of the most creative educational reformers of all time: He published one of the first illustrated children's textbooks, created graded education, and introduced student-centered learning. Yet he is best known for being the first to advocate for universal education based on the simple theological truth that all humans are made in God's image. Interestingly, Comenius would be invited to become president of a new college that had just started in the American colonies called Harvard.[26] Unfortunately, he never came, but others in America still set forth the revolutionary implications of being made in God's image.

The Early American Vision

In 1765, the president of Yale College, Thomas Clap (1703–1767), published one of the first college textbooks printed in America. The text was meant for the capstone course taught at all existing American colleges at the time: moral philosophy. This course was considered so important that it was always taught by the college's president. What was the central point of this most important course in the curriculum? Clap insisted, "As Man was at first made in the moral Image or Likeness to God [Gen. 1:26–27], so the recovery of that Image is the greatest duty and highest perfection."[27] Clearly, Clap was familiar with the Christian tradition's historic emphasis on this central purpose of education.

This teaching would make it into the bestselling schoolbook used in the late seventeenth and throughout the eighteenth century, *The New*

25. Comenius, *Great Didactic*, 68.

26. J. H. Blodgett, "Was Comenius Called to the Presidency of Harvard?," *Educational Review* 8 (1898).

27. Thomas Clap, *An Essay on the Nature and Foundation of Moral Virtue and Obligation: Being a Short Introduction to the Study of Ethics; For the Use of the Students of Yale-College* (B. Mecom, 1765), 54.

England Primer. The *Primer* included the Westminster Shorter Catechism, which contained this question: "*Q. 35. What is sanctification?* A. Sanctification is the work of God's free grace, whereby we are renewed in the whole man, after the image of God, and are enabled more and more to die unto sin, and live unto righteousness."[28] Education was then understood to contribute to the renewal of the image of God.

Interestingly, even the major advocate of public schools in America, Horace Mann (1796–1859), who was not even an orthodox Christian (he was Unitarian), recognized that all humans are made in God's image. He also, at one point, acknowledged that the full development of humans made in God's image was the end of education. He made this point through setting forth an imaginary exercise for his audience that brought home the importance of education: "If, instead of twenty-one *years*, the course of Nature allowed but twenty-one *days*, to rear an infant to the full stature of manhood, and to sow in his bosom, the seeds of unbounded happiness or of unspeakable misery, I suppose, in that case, the merchant would abandon his bargains, and the farmer would leave the in-gathering of his harvest, and even the drunkard would head homeward from the midst of his revel, and *that* twenty-one days would be spent, without much sleep, and with many prayers."[29]

He then shared what the consequences of a "vicious education" would be at the end of this twenty-one days: "His tongue were already roughened with oaths and blasphemy; or he were seen skulking through society, obtaining credit upon false pretenses, or with rolls of counterfeit bills in his pocket; or were already expiating his offences in the bondage and infamy of a prison." In contrast, a virtuous education would lead to a "majestic" young person "who [was] possessed of all those qualities and attributes, which a being created in the image of God *ought to have*."[30]

Mann understood that the view that humans are made in God's image provides a purpose and obligation for human development. The end of education is to restore the image of God in humanity, with the central virtues being the excellences God demonstrated in Scripture.

28. *The New England Primer* (Philadelphia, 1777), n.p.
29. Horace Mann, *Lectures on Education* (Ide and Dutton, 1855), 16.
30. Mann, *Lectures on Education*, 16–17.

Unfortunately, this understanding and rationale for education would slowly disappear from American education. The first major institutions of higher education, Harvard, William and Mary, Yale, Princeton, Dartmouth, and Brown, although started as Christian, would slowly secularize.[31] In addition, although Horace Mann started a nonsectarian K–12 public education system that still included prayer and devotional Bible reading, the public K–12 system would also slowly secularize as well.[32] One scholar, who did a systematic review of K–12 curriculum and various higher education programs, concluded, "Most public schools and universities border on secular indoctrination (and many cross the line). In doing so, they encourage (secular) faith."[33] Certainly, they no longer understand all students as image bearers of God who need to recover and grow in the full understanding of that image and make that their "entire task" and "greatest duty."

31. George Marsden, *The Soul of the American University: From Protestant to Postsecular* (Oxford University Press, 2021).

32. Warren A. Nord, *Does God Make a Difference? Taking Religion Seriously in Our Schools and Universities* (Oxford University Press, 2010).

33. Nord, *Does God Make a Difference?*, 94.

CHAPTER SEVEN

The Image of God, Political Liberty, and the Abolition of Slavery

> Rights and dignity can be real only if human beings are more than biological matter. The modern secular discourse on human rights depends on retaining in some fashion—but without acknowledging—the belief that every human being is created in the image and likeness of God.
>
> —Brad Gregory[1]

One of the most shameful developments in the history of biblical interpretation pertains to the story of the curse of Ham found in Genesis 9:20–25. The unusual story gives a recounting of one incident Noah had with his sons after the flood:

> Noah, a man of the soil, proceeded to plant a vineyard. When he drank some of its wine, he became drunk and lay uncovered inside his tent. Ham, the father of Canaan, saw his father naked and told his two brothers

1. Brad Gregory, *The Unintended Reformation: How a Religious Revolution Secularized Society* (Harvard University Press, 2012), 381.

> outside. But Shem and Japheth took a garment and laid it across their shoulders; then they walked in backward and covered their father's naked body. Their faces were turned the other way so that they would not see their father naked. When Noah awoke from his wine and found out what his youngest son had done to him, he said,
>
> "Cursed be Canaan!
> The lowest of slaves
> will he be to his brothers."

Unfortunately, as one scholar noted, "This Biblical story has been the single greatest justification for Black slavery for more than a thousand years. It is a strange justification indeed, for there is no reference in it to Blacks at all."[2]

Oddly, the origins of the faulty biblical interpretation, that the curse related to skin color, came about in the seventh century at the time of the Islamic conquests in northern Africa and southern Asia. Islamist scholars began categorizing people groups by skin color.[3] Certain Islamic writers also began to describe Ham's curse as one involving both slavery and black skin color.[4] Sadly, the spread of this story also corresponded to the increasing enslavement of Black Africans in the Islamic empire.

Unfortunately, this problematic interpretation eventually made its way into Christian thinking through Eastern Christian sources in the ninth century.[5] Moreover, the important Christian counter to this problematic interpretation did not arise until seven centuries later. Besides noting that the story of Ham does not mention skin color, the Christian argument against this kind of dehumanization came from thinkers who drew on Scripture's positive message regarding humanity. They reached back to Genesis 1 to recognize that skin hue does not make anyone more or less an image bearer of God or a human created by God.

In addition, Christians started to recognize that Paul's sermon to the Athenians in Acts 17 emphasized that God made all humans from one

2. David M. Goldenberg, *The Curse of Ham: Race and Slavery in Early Judaism, Christianity, and Islam* (Princeton University Press, 2003), 1.

3. Bernard Lewis, *Race and Slavery in the Middle East: An Historical Inquiry* (Oxford University Press, 1992).

4. Goldenberg, *Curse of Ham*, 170.

5. Goldenberg, *Curse of Ham*.

blood. They realized that meant we all have the same origin, personhood, and value. Skin color does not determine whether one is made in God's image. Abolitionists, those arguing for the end of slavery, used these biblical teachings to argue for both the humanity of Black Africans and the inhumanity of slavery. This chapter chronicles the historical progression of these arguments as well as the influence this outlook had on human understandings of political liberty in general.

God Hath Made of One Blood All Nations

In 1526, William Tyndale completed his groundbreaking translation of the English New Testament. In this translation, Tyndale employed a unique phrase that was not present in John Wycliffe's original late fourteenth-century English translation of the Bible. Instead of translating a key passage from Paul's sermon to the Athenians in Wycliffe's original way, "[God] made of one all the kind of men" (Acts 17:26a), Tyndale translated the verse "[God] hath made of one bloud all nacions of men for to dwell on all the face of the erthe."[6] The King James would translate the passage in the same (albeit more readable) way for contemporaries: "[God] hath made of one blood all nations [Greek: *ethnos*] of men for to dwell on all the face of the earth." A little more than a century later, this simple English sentence, especially when combined with the key idea that all humans are made in God's image, would begin to have enormous implications for the abolition of Black slavery.

The transformation began with the practice of Puritan pastors in early 1600s England, who expounded on the ramifications of this passage for our social relationships. First, pastors started to realize in light of Acts 17:26a that "in regard of body and birth, there is no difference originally betwixt man and man"[7] and that everyone is one's neighbor.[8] Others

6. Apart from this quote, I modified all other quotes from old English in this chapter to modern English.

7. William Perkins, *A Commentary upon the 11th Chapter to the Hebrews* (Leonard Green, 1613), 47.

8. Henry Ainsworth, *A Commentary upon the Second Book of Moses Called Exodus* (1617), n.p. (Exod. 20:17).

recognized this meant that the poor man "is a man of my own nature"[9] and "made of the same mold, hewed out of the same rock thou was, nay, he is thine own flesh (as the Prophet speaks) for 'we are all made but of one blood' (Acts 17:26)."[10]

In other words, they began to recognize the humanity of those on the margins of society. In 1635, the Scottish Reformed minister John Weemes, mentioned in chapter 5, would apply this passage to humans with different skin colors. He wrote, "For as, All men were created of one blood, Acts 17 [26a], but accidentally they differ in their skin color."[11] By "accidentally," he simply meant, "Their color varies in respect of the climate under which they dwell."[12] Paul's retelling of God's creation of humans in his image established this emerging Christian understanding of who was fully human and deserving of love and respect. From that point forward, we find additional references to the one-blood argument as a counter to African dehumanization and slavery.

God's Image in Ebony

Near the same time, the truth that Black people are also made in God's image began to be more widely proclaimed. In 1642, the Anglican minister and church historian Thomas Fuller made one of the first known descriptions of dark-skinned people as made in God's image in a book titled *The Holy State*.[13]

His book described how a Christian should be excellent in various personal and professional identities (the subject of chapter 12 in this book). In one chapter, he described the good ship captain. One of the challenges of the good ship captain was that he led a government war vessel. Thus, he had to decide what to do with captured pirates or other

9. Archibald Symmer, *A Spirituall Posie for Zion* (London, 1629), 5.

10. Richard Bernard, *A Ready Way to Good Works* (London, 1635), 143.

11. John Weemes, *Observations Naturall and Morall*, in *The Collected Works of Mr. John Weemes*, vol. 1 (1637), 26.

12. Weemes, *Observations Naturall and Morall*.

13. Thomas Fuller, *The Holy State* (Cambridge, 1642), https://quod.lib.umich.edu/e/eebo/A40674.0001.001/1:8.21?rgn=div2;view=toc. The language is modified to suit modern-day English.

prisoners of war. Here, Fuller described, using theological reasoning, what the good ship captain does:

> *In taking a prize he most prizeth the men's lives whom he takes;* though some of them may chance to be Negroes or Savages. 'Tis the custom of some to cast them overboard, and there's an end of them: for the dumb fishes will tell no tales. But the murder is not so soon drowned as the men. What, is a brother by the half blood no kin? A Savage hath God to his father by creation, though not the Church to his mother, and God will revenge his innocent blood. But our Captain counts the image of God nevertheless his image cut in ebony as if done in ivory, and in the blackest Moores, he sees the representation of the King of heaven.[14]

For Fuller, the good ship captain recognizes that all humans, including "the blackest Moores," are God's image "cut in ebony," and therefore their lives should be preserved. To be clear, however, these arguments were not yet used to argue against slavery. That would come later.

Humans of One Blood Made in God's Image

A decade later, both "image of God" and "one blood" language would be used by government officials to form a theological foundation for human worth and dignity that did not rest simply on the choices of a government. In 1645, English Puritans, led by Oliver Cromwell, deposed Charles I for what they saw as his repressive policies. They then began to use both the one-blood argument and the claim that we are made in God's image to argue against domestic and foreign political oppression.

Puritan thinkers, for example, began to appeal to the doctrine of the image of God to affirm the humanity of political subjects in the face of monarchist claims. John Milton (1608–1674), the famous author of *Paradise Lost* and *Paradise Regained*, was perhaps the first to make this appeal in 1651. Against those defending Charles I and the divine right of kings, Milton wrote *A Defence of the People of England*. In this work, Milton would make the following defense of human liberty against political tyrants and slavery:

14. Fuller, *Holy State*, 8.228.

> Our liberty is not Caesar's; tis a blessing we have received from God himself; tis what we are born to; to lay this down at Caesar's feet which we derive not from him, which we are not beholden to him for, were an unworthy action, a degrading of our very Nature. If one should consider attentively the countenance of a man, and enquire after whose Image so noble a Creature were framed; would not any one that heard him, presently make answer, that he was made after the image of God himself? Being therefore peculiarly God's own; we are entirely free by Nature, and cannot without the greatest sacrilege imaginable be reduced into a condition of slavery to any man, especially to a wicked, unjust cruel tyrant.[15]

Milton recognized that, because we are created in God's image, we have been gifted political freedom. Moreover, he understood that this means political authority does not endow us with freedoms that can be arbitrarily taken away by the government. Our freedom from political slavery is given by God.

Four years later, in 1655, a declaration made under Oliver Cromwell's name (but written by John Milton) used the one-blood argument in a declaration against Spain's mistreatment of Native Americans. The declaration argued, "Since God hath made of one blood all nations of men, for to dwell on all the face of the earth, and hath determined the times before appointed, and the bounds of their habitation; and at one time or another, God will have an account of the innocent blood of so many millions of Indians, so barbarously butchered by the Spaniards, and of the wrong and injustice that hath been done unto them."[16] As can be seen, an emerging pattern of thought and practice was established by these Puritans. They used both Genesis 1:26 and Paul's Acts 17 "one blood" reference to argue for the equality of all humanity, including the poor, one's enemy, humans of various skin colors, and Native Americans.

These arguments for basing human dignity on the fact that we are made in the image of God would continue to expand in ways that would have implications for the American Revolution and its founders' exaltation of equal human rights in the face of tyranny. For instance, the

15. John Milton, *A Defence of the People of England* (Amsterdam, 1692), 56.

16. John Milton, "Extracts from Oliver Cromwell's Declaration Against Spain (1655)," *London Magazine* 9 (1740): 448.

most influential English thinker writing about human rights, John Locke (1632–1704), would use this doctrine in his *First Treatise* (1689).[17] He argued against the belief that only certain men were given dominion over the earth. In contrast, Locke argued that Scripture shows "God, in this donation, gave the world to mankind [i.e., humanity] in common, and not to *Adam* in particular. The word *them* in the text must include the species of man, for it is certain *them* can by no means signify *Adam* alone. In the 26th verse, where God declares his intention to give this dominion, it is plain he meant, that he would make a species of creatures, that should have dominion over the other species of this terrestrial globe."[18] Based on this doctrine, Locke would go on to offer an even more expansive argument that all humans, including women, have God-given natural rights over and against the government.

The Use of the Image of God and the One-Blood Arguments to Argue Against Slavery

Although all these arguments made clear that the image of God applied to all humanity, it only later began to be applied to Black African slaves. Not surprisingly, when you compare the arguments of the Christians supporting the abolition of slavery to the Christian defenders of slavery from the 1600s to the early 1800s, you find that the former constantly focused on the doctrine that all humans are made in God's image and that we are all made from one blood, while the defenders ignored it.

Those in favor of abolishing slavery first argued that we must recognize African Americans' equal humanity and right to religion. For example, Morgan Godwyn (1640–ca. 1686), an English Anglican from the seventeenth century who was once King Charles I's personal priest, wrote in his 1685 book *Negro's and Indians Advocate* that we should view Black people and Native Americans as image bearers of God who deserve a right to religion since we can see "our Blessed Savior in the

17. For more on this topic, see Roger Ruston, *Human Rights and the Image of God* (SCM, 2004), 210.

18. John Locke, *Two Treatises of Government* (London, 1690), 37–38, emphasis original.

Negro's complexion."[19] In contrast, he observed that those who want to deny the humanity of Black people and Native Americans resorted to silly arguments to deny Genesis 1:27, such as claiming that other races were created outside of Adam or that their allegedly bestial behavior undermines their humanity (sadly, one adherent to these silly arguments was Thomas Jefferson[20]). Through such arguments, they "throw off all respect for the work of God's hand."[21]

Soon, others took these arguments further. The first antislavery treatise published on American soil was written by the Quaker George Keith to his fellow Quakers in 1693. He began his caution against buying slaves by reminding his readers "that Negroes, Blacks, and Tannies are a real part of Mankind, for whom Christ hath shed his precious blood and capable of salvation" and that they, too, "bear his image."[22] The argument started with the key point that all humans are made in God's image.

This same argument would emerge again in the second known antislavery publication in the American colonies. The author, Samuel Sewall (1652–1730), was labeled "a typical Massachusetts Puritan"[23] by one early biographer, but in one respect, he was anything but. He penned the first antislavery tract in America that appealed to the whole colonial audience (the first publication appealed only to Quakers). Sewall published the tract "The Selling of Joseph" (1700) after finding out that a Boston judge was planning to keep an indentured servant as a lifelong slave.[24] Indentured servants were to be released after a period of time. Thus,

19. Morgan Godwyn, *The Negro's & Indians Advocate, Suing for Their Admission into the Church, or, A Persuasive to the Instructing and Baptizing of the Negro's and Indians in Our Plantations Shewing, That as the Compliance Therewith Can Prejudice No Man's Just Interest: So the Wilful Neglecting and Opposing of It, Is No Less than a Manifest Apostacy from the Christian Faith; To Which Is Added, a Brief Account of Religion in Virginia* (Printed for the author, by J. D., 1680), 21.

20. Thomas Jefferson, *Notes on the State of Virginia*, 2nd ed. (Philadelphia, 1794).

21. Godwyn, *Negro's & Indians Advocate*, 21.

22. George Keith, "An Exhortation and Caution to Friends Concerning Buying or Keeping of Negroes," 1693, Huntington Digital Library, https://hdl.huntington.org/digital/collection/p16003coll17/id/29837/.

23. John Louis Ewell, *Judge Samuel Sewall, 1652–1730 a Typical Massachusetts Puritan* (Knickerbocker Press, 1895).

24. Samuel Sewall, "The Selling of Joseph: A Memorial (1700)," University of Nebraska-Lincoln, Electronic Texts in American Studies, accessed November 9, 2025, https://digitalcommons.unl.edu/etas/26.

he began by declaring, "It is most certain that all Men, as they are the Sons of Adam, are Coheirs; and have equal Right unto Liberty, and all other outward Comforts of Life. God hath given the Earth (with all its Commodities) unto the Sons of Adam, Psal 115. 16. And hath made of One Blood, all Nations of Men, for to dwell on all the face of the Earth; and hath determined the Times before appointed, and the bounds of their habitation."[25]

He would go on to close his argument with these words: "These Ethiopians, as black as they are; seeing they are the Sons and Daughters of the First Adam, the Brethren and Sister of the Last Adam, and the offspring of GOD; They ought to be treated with a Respect agreeable." His 1895 biographer observed that he backed up his words throughout his life: "Nineteen years later, when a grandson of his and the daughter of a negro wood-chopper were baptized together in his church, he wrote in his diary, 'so all are one in Christ.'"[26]

To be clear, most Puritan Christians in America during this time did not see the belief that all humans are equally made in God's image (Gen. 1:26) from one blood (Acts 17:26) as completely forbidding slavery, even though they concluded we are all equal before God. Unfortunately, most did not equate equality before God with requiring equal legal respect and freedom for all humans. Sewall was an exception. Yet Puritans' adherence to the Bible did create the possibility for some key leaders to begin emphasizing equal moral respect for all humanity that led to later abolitionist arguments.

The third known American antislavery tract demonstrates this progression. In 1715 John Hepburn wrote that it is not often "that I appear in print, but my Christian duty in honor to God, and the salvation and well-being of the souls of men, is the detestation of the anti-Christian practice in making slaves of them who bear the image of God, viz, their fellow Creature."[27] From that time forward, we find both the "image of

25. Sewall, "Selling of Joseph," 1.

26. Ewell, *Judge Samuel Sewall*, 39.

27. John Hepburn, *The American Defense of the Christian Golden Rule or an Essay to Prove the Unlawfulness of Making Slaves of Men* (London, 1715), in *Evans Early American Imprint Collection*, University of Michigan Library Digital Collections, accessed July 8, 2025, https://name.umdl.umich.edu/N01412.0001.001. See also Henry J. Cadbury, "John Hepburn and His Book Against Slavery," *Proceedings of the American Antiquarian Society* 59, no. 1 (1949): 89–113.

God" and "one blood" arguments used repeatedly by famous abolitionists such as the Quaker John Woolman (1754) and one of the founders of Methodism, John Wesley (1774).[28]

American Arguments for Equal Human Rights

As we saw with John Milton earlier, the arguments for political liberty from a repressive state and the arguments against slavery both shared a common appeal to the image of God. For instance, the call of early American founders for the state to respect the natural rights of humans was also based on this Christian doctrine. Thomas Paine, the founder as far from Christian orthodoxy as any, still referred to Genesis 1:27 in his famous work *The Rights of Man* to support his argument that all "are born equal and with equal natural right."[29] He based this claim on the biblical text: "'And God said, let us make man in our own image: in the image of God created he him—*male* and *female* created he them.' The distinction of sexes is pointed out, but no other distinction is even implied. If this be not divine authority, it is historical authority and shows that the quality of man, so far from being a modern doctrine, is the oldest upon record."[30]

Although Thomas Jefferson would later famously write, "We hold these truths to be self-evident that all men are created equal," the reality is that this truth was not always self-evident. It took Christians emphasizing the doctrine that all humans are created in God's image and made of one blood to begin to make its social implications clear. Indeed, sadly, Jefferson himself did not expand this supposedly "self-evident" doctrine to include African Americans. It would take others to do that.

One important individual to make this argument was Lemuel Haynes (1753–1833), the first Black American officially ordained as a minister. He argued in his 1776 tract "Liberty Further Extended" that "a Negro may justly challenge, and has an undeniable right to his Liberty. Consequently,

28. John Woolman, *Some Considerations on the Keeping of Negroes: Recommended to the Professors of Christianity of Every Denomination* (Tract Association of Friends, 1754), 2; John Wesley, *Thoughts upon Slavery* (London, 1774), 57.

29. Thomas Paine, *The Rights of Man* (London, 1795), 7.

30. Paine, *Rights of Man*, 7.

the practice of Slave-keeping, which so much abounds in this land is illicit."[31] The basis of his argument was grounded on this passage: "'It hath pleased God to *make of one Blood all nations of men, for to dwell upon the face of the Earth*.' Acts 17, 26–23. And as all are of one species, so there are the same laws, and aspiring principles placed in all nations; and the effect that these laws will produce, are similar to each other."[32]

This biblical appeal later shaped numerous American abolitionists' arguments. In his book *Of One Blood: Abolitionism and the Origins of Racial Equality*, Paul Goodman observed, "The underpinning of their [the abolitionists'] views was Christian faith in the unity of mankind: 'God hath created of one blood all nations of men for to dwell on the face of the earth.' To elevate one race over another because of color, hair texture, lip thickness, or nose shape introduced arbitrary and invidious man-made distinctions into God's creation. Such prejudice was tantamount to blasphemy, they argued, for it degraded part of God's creation for selfish, prideful, exploitative purposes."[33] Thus, one finds declarations such as the following required among early abolitionist societies: "We believe, and would do all in our power to convince others, that 'God hath made of one blood all nations of men for to dwell on all the face of the earth.'"[34] They would also question new members whether they believed the one-blood doctrine.

In addition, the doctrine of the image of God played a central role in the abolitionist argument. As David Brion Davis noted in his book *Image of God: Religion, Moral Values, and Our Heritage of Slavery*, "The popular hostility to slavery that emerged almost simultaneously in England and in parts of the United States drew upon the tradition of natural law and a revivified sense of the image of God in man."[35]

31. Lemuel Haynes, "Liberty Further Extended: Or Free Thoughts on the Illegality of Slave-Keeping; Wherein Those Arguments That Are Used in Its Vindication Are Plainly Confuted; Together with an Humble Address to Such as Are Concerned in the Practice (1776)," University of Nebraska-Lincoln, Electronic Texts in American Studies, accessed November 10, 2025, https://digitalcommons.unl.edu/etas/94.

32. Haynes, "Liberty Further Extended," emphasis original.

33. Paul Goodman, *Of One Blood: Abolitionism and the Origins of Racial Equality* (University of California Press, 1998), 58.

34. Goodman, *Of One Blood*, 132.

35. David Brion Davis, *Image of God: Religion, Moral Values, and Our Heritage of Slavery* (Yale University Press, 2001), 198. See also Deirdre N. McCloskey,

This biblical appeal would continue for the next two centuries. As the Southern abolitionist Angelina Grimké argued in 1836, humanity "who was created in the image of his Maker, *never* can properly be termed a *thing*, though the laws of Slave States do call him 'a chattel personal.'"[36]

Similarly, the famous African American abolitionist Frederick Douglass proclaimed when discussing the nature of slavery,

> The physical cruelties are indeed sufficiently harassing and revolting; but they are as a few grains of sand on the ocean, compared with the stupendous wrongs which it inflicts upon the mental, moral, and religious nature of its hapless victims. . . . The slave is a man, "the image of God," but "a little lower than the angels"; possessing a soul, eternal and indestructible, capable of endless happiness, immeasurable woe; a creature of hopes and fears, of affections and passions, of joys and sorrows; and he is endowed with those mysterious powers by which man soars above the things of time and sense, and grasps, with undying tenacity, the elevating and sublimely glorious idea of a God.[37]

He argued, "This is why slavery of any kind is an outrage. It spoils the image of God as it strives to express itself through the individual or the race."[38]

Eventually, through abolitionists such as Frederick Douglass, the social and political implications of what it means for all humans to be made in God's image began to be recognized. Unfortunately, this recognition occurred primarily in the North. It took a bloody civil war for Christians in the South to give up slavery. We must always remember that Christians sometimes place their economic interests above God's truth.

Unfortunately, after the Civil War many Southerners did not give up treating Black people as less than fully human bearers of God's image. For example, in 1900, a man named Charles Carroll spent $20,000 of

---

Bourgeois Equality: How Ideas, Not Capital or Institutions, Enriched the World (University of Chicago Press, 2016).

36. Angelina Emily Grimké, *Appeal to Christian Women of the South* (New York, 1836), 3.

37. Frederick Douglass, "The Nature of Slavery," in *African-American Social and Political Thought, 1850–1920*, ed. Howard Brotz (Transaction, 1992), 217.

38. Frederick Douglass, "The African Problem and the Method of Its Solution," in *African-American Social and Political Thought, 1850–1920*, ed. Howard Brotz (Transaction, 1992), 138.

his money to publish the horrific book *"The Negro a Beast" or "In the Image of God."* Carroll claimed to offer "convincing biblical and scientific evidence that the Negro is not of the human family."[39] His book is just one such effort. It would take a peaceful movement later in the twentieth century to directly counter such arguments and begin the process of addressing the unjust treatment of African Americans. Once again, this movement would rely on both the image of God and one-blood arguments.

The Civil Rights Movement and Martin Luther King Jr.

It comes as no surprise that Martin Luther King Jr., the leader of the civil rights movement, relied heavily on the doctrine of the image of God in his advocacy for civil rights for African Americans. Richard Wayne Wills, in his book about King's use of this key doctrine, argues that King's understanding of the image of God had four key elements:

> First, all individuals, as children of God, were equally valued inasmuch as they were birthed with an inherent dignity. Second, human beings had an intrinsic worth that in and of itself became the requisite for the bestowal of just and fair treatment. Third, in addition to warranting just treatment by virtue of their having been created in the image of God, humanity thus created possessed the capacity to cooperate with God by living out the mandates of their moral conscience, such that the desire to choose to do that which is socially good can actually be translated into the deed itself. Fourth and finally, the image of God provided the existential common ground for genuine community-building, making beloved community, in its broadest sense, a distinct historical possibility.[40]

In Martin Luther King Jr. we finally see the full and wide-ranging application of the image of God to social and political thought.

39. Charles Carroll, *"The Negro a Beast" or "In the Image of God"* (American Book and Bible House, 1900), 6.

40. Richard W. Wills, *Martin Luther King Jr. and the Image of God* (Oxford University Press, 2009), 113. I should note one major weakness with this volume: Wills unfortunately misinterprets how numerous church fathers and Reformers understood the image of God in this book, claiming that many of them thought the image of God was completely lost after the fall.

What made King's understanding even more powerful is that he applied it not only to his own race but to the enemies of his race. King had numerous enemies, constantly received hate mail, and often experienced death threats. Indeed, he died at the hands of a murderer. Nonetheless, King constantly preached about how even these enemies should be treated with love since they are image bearers of God.

In his famous sermon "Loving Your Enemies," he pointed out how this doctrine plays a key role in remembering the humanity of your enemy: "And when you come to the point that you look in the face of every man and see deep down within him . . . 'the image of God,' you begin to love him in spite of. No matter what he does, you see God's image there. There is an element of goodness that he can never slough off. Discover the element of good in your enemy."[41] As King recognized, when we view others first as image bearers of God and not as our enemies, we find the ability to do what Jesus commanded us to do: "But I tell you, love your enemies and pray for those who persecute you" (Matt. 5:44). An important step in fulfilling that command is seeing your enemies as image bearers of God.

Today, we still need to unpack and consider what it means that all humans are made in God's image and what it means to restore that defaced image. All over the world, we find the dehumanization of those who are different from us. They may be groups from other tribes (e.g., the Hutu killing of Tutsis in the Rwandan genocide), religious ethnic groups (e.g., the mistreatment of the Muslim Uyghurs by the Chinese government, the killing of Christians by Islamists in Nigeria and Syria), or historically oppressed groups (e.g., the reemergence of anti-Semitism).

We also need to be on guard continuously against replacing the truth that all humans are made in God's image with popular theories that neglect this point. Theories that appear to address social injustice but do not begin with the affirmation that we are made in God's image often

41. Martin Luther King Jr., "'Loving Your Enemies,' Sermon Delivered at Dexter Avenue Baptist Church," The Martin Luther King, Jr. Research and Education Institute, accessed November 10, 2025, https://kinginstitute.stanford.edu/king-papers/documents/loving-your-enemies-sermon-delivered-dexter-avenue-baptist-church.

only reproduce tribalism that leads to the dehumanization of the other. They offer us no meta-identity that can be a source of worth and dignity for every human.

The next chapter explores what this reality means for our lives and how we treat others. Then, the rest of part 4 explores how recognizing that you are made in God's image should also lead to three other key realizations. First, you need to know God and his character before you can truly understand your purpose. Second, you need to recognize why humans do not currently image God's character. Finally, you need to know how to become most fully human—which, not surprisingly, starts with God's actions toward you but must continue with your actions toward him.

PART IV

The Image of God and Contemporary Application

We can learn a lot from idiots. The one I have in mind is Lev Nikolayevich Myshkin, the titular protagonist from Fyodor Dostoyevsky's *The Idiot*. In one part of the book, Myshkin recounts a story to a group of high-society partygoers about Marie, the daughter of a disabled person who was seduced by a French traveler and then abandoned. Consequently, "She came home dirty, draggled, and shoeless; she had walked for a whole week without shoes; she had slept in the fields and caught a terrible cold; her feet were swollen and sore, and her hands torn and scratched all over."[1] Notice the language used to describe the adults' treatment of her: "Everyone standing around looked at her as if she was a reptile; the old men condemned and scolded her, the young people laughed, the women shouted abuse at her and glared at her as if she was some kind of loathsome spider."[2] A reptile and a spider.

1. Fyodor Dostoyevsky, *The Idiot*, trans. Henry and Olga Carlisle (Signet, 1980), 88.
2. Dostoyevsky, *The Idiot*, 89.

The dehumanization became even worse after Marie's mother died. "Then they stopped giving Marie anything to eat at all; and in the village everyone chased her off, and no one would give her work, as they had done before. Everyone virtually spat on her, the men no longer even treated her as a woman, and they would say obscene things to her."[3] Given the beastly treatment from the adults, it is no surprise that the village's forty schoolchildren teased her and threw mud at her.

The Idiot then begins his lessons in Christian education. He shared how, although he had little money, he sold a diamond to give Marie money. He attempted to kiss her hand when he gave her the money, but she pulled it away. The children, seeing all this, act as children do. They made fun of Myshkin and Marie and threw mud at both. They continued their torments. "The children would not let her pass now in the streets but annoyed her and threw dirt at her more than before. They used to run after her—she racing away with her poor feeble lungs panting and gasping, and they pelted her and shouted abuse at her." Myshkin related, "Once I had to interfere by force; and after that I took to speaking to them every day and whenever I could. Occasionally, they stopped and listened, but they teased Marie all the same."[4]

Myshkin then became the children's moral educator. He began, as a good moral educator should, by telling the children Marie's story to shape their affections and stir their compassion: "I told them how unhappy Marie was, and after a while, they stopped their abuse of her and let her go by silently. Little by little we got into the way of conversing together, the children and me. I concealed nothing from them, I told them all. They listened very attentively and soon began to be sorry for Marie."[5]

Through his stories, Myshkin influenced and shaped the children's affections and empathy. Only then did the children apply the manners they had already learned from other adults: "At last some of them took to saying 'Good-morning' to her, kindly, when they met her. It is the custom there to salute anyone you meet with 'Good-morning' whether acquainted or not. I can imagine how astonished Marie was at these

3. Dostoyevsky, *The Idiot*, 89.
4. Dostoyevsky, *The Idiot*, 90.
5. Dostoyevsky, *The Idiot*, 91.

first greetings from the children."[6] Myshkin had helped Marie, a reptile and spider in the eyes of the adults, become human in the eyes of the children.

As a result, the children became more human as well. They started showing hospitality to Marie. "Once two little girls got hold of some food and took it to her and came back and told me. They said she had burst into tears, and that they loved her very much now."[7] Suddenly, the extreme gratitude for this simple act of kindness changed the girls' hearts. The girls then led the other children. "Very soon after that they all became fond of Marie, and at the same time they began to develop the greatest affection for myself. They often came to me and begged me to tell them stories. I think I must have told stories well, for they did so love to hear them."[8]

The children even persisted in their humane treatment in the face of the adults' inhumanity: "Everyone discovered now that the little ones had taken to being fond of Marie, and their parents were terribly alarmed; but Marie was so happy. The children were forbidden to meet her."[9] The inhumanity of parents wanting to protect their children from imagined evils always proves a powerful motivation for dehumanizing others.

The children, however, knew what was good, as the Idiot tells us, "They used to run out of the village to the herd and take her food and things; and sometimes just ran off there and kissed her, and said, '*Je vous aime*, Marie!' and then trotted back again. They imagined that I was in love with Marie, and this was the only point on which I did not undeceive them, for they got such enjoyment out of it. And what delicacy and tenderness they showed!"[10] The children had moved from showing good manners to showing kindness and tenderness.

It did not stop there: "When we left her, Marie used to relapse at once into her old condition and sit with closed eyes and motionless limbs. One day she could not go out at all and remained at home all alone in the empty hut; but the children very soon became aware of the fact, and nearly all of them visited her that day as she lay alone and helpless in

6. Dostoyevsky, *The Idiot*, 91.
7. Dostoyevsky, *The Idiot*, 91.
8. Dostoyevsky, *The Idiot*, 91.
9. Dostoyevsky, *The Idiot*, 92.
10. Dostoyevsky, *The Idiot*, 92.

her miserable bed."[11] The children moved from simple acts of kindness to following Christ's command to visit the sick and treat them as if they were Christ himself. Their moral heroism finally aroused the adults to some humanity:

> For two days the children looked after her, and then, when the village people got to know that Marie was really dying, some of the old women came and took it in turns to sit by her and look after her a bit. I think they began to be a little sorry for her in the village at last; at all events they did not interfere with the children anymore, on her account.
>
> Marie lay in a state of uncomfortable delirium the whole while; she coughed dreadfully. The old women would not let the children stay in the room; but they all collected outside the window each morning, if only for a moment, and shouted '*Bon jour, notre bonne Marie!*' and Marie no sooner caught sight of, or heard them, and she became quite animated at once, and, in spite of the old women, would try to sit up and nod her head and smile at them, and thank them. The little ones used to bring her nice things and sweets to eat, but she could hardly touch anything. Thanks to them, I assure you, the girl died almost perfectly happy.[12]

Not only did Marie become human in their eyes but the children and the adults also slowly became the humans they were meant to be. They had experienced a particular kind of moral education. They had moved from beastly vice, to recognizing that Marie was an image bearer of God, to then showing her his virtues, as image bearers of God themselves. I would venture that the author of *Forrest Gump* gained some inspiration from this *Idiot*.[13] So should we.

We all need to learn how to recognize and unleash the image of God in everyone, including ourselves. The fourth part of this book will discuss what it would look like in our contemporary society to move from recognizing the image of God in ourselves and others to then acquiring the character qualities of God that help us restore that defaced image.

11. Dostoyevsky, *The Idiot*, 93.
12. Dostoyevsky, *The Idiot*, 93.
13. Winston Groom, *Forrest Gump* (Vintage, 2012).

CHAPTER EIGHT

Recognizing Our Own and Others' Human Worth and Dignity

> This is scary: You can tame a tiger, but you can't tame a tongue—it's never been done. The tongue runs wild, a wanton killer. With our tongues we bless God our Father; with the same tongues we curse the very men and women he made in his image.
>
> —James 3:9–10 (MSG)

As a Baylor University professor, I was excited when the Baylor men's basketball team won the national championship in 2021. Yet I was even more proud of how they won it. Coach Scott Drew led the team in building a culture of JOY: Jesus, Others, and Yourself. You would notice how they demonstrated that culture even in their interviews. First, they would point to God, then compliment their teammates or coaches, and only then would they talk about themselves.

Another way the coaches implemented this culture was in helping the players understand their worth. An example of how this worked came from Jared Butler, a current NBA basketball player. While attending Baylor University, he was named the preseason Big 12 Player of the Year and was spoken of as a future NBA player. Thus, he faced significant pressure to play up to that expectation. It was easily a situation where he could have put his worth in how well he performed on the basketball court. He confessed, "I think a lot of times for me I put a lot of pressure on myself to perform and live up to this name that people have put on me."[1]

To address this pressure, the coaching staff helped Butler realize something he later told ESPN magazine: "But I think at the end of the day, it's about what my Lord and Savior says about me, not about what any person or any ESPN rating or any NBA draft or NBA player says about me. It's about what He says."[2]

Later that year, after making those remarks, Butler and his teammates would go on to win the NCAA national championship. In his case, this attitude freed him up to perform with excellence at the highest level. It should be no surprise that there are numerous cases of elite athletes or musicians performing better once they realize their worth does not come from their performance.[3] In fact, researchers have found that athletes with a secure source of worth in God had the lowest levels of mental health illness indicators and the highest life satisfaction.[4]

This reality, however, does not simply relate to elite athletes. It applies to everyone because every human is made in God's image. As the Hebrew scholar Ari Lamm notes, "Every single descendant of Adam and Eve possesses equal and intrinsic worth in God's eyes. None of us bears more of God's image than any other."[5] This chapter will outline the contemporary implications of not only finding your worth in God but also seeing others as made in his image—including your enemies.

1. As quoted in Will Chamblee, "Big 12 Player of the Year Jared Butler Deals with Pressures in a Unique Way," *The Baylor Lariat*, January 20, 2021.

2. As quoted in Chamblee, "Big 12 Player of the Year."

3. Benjamin Houltberg, Kenneth T. Wang, Wei Qi, and Christina S. Nelson, "Self-Narrative Profiles of Elite Athletes and Comparisons on Psychological Well-Being," *Research Quarterly for Exercise and Sport* 89, no. 3 (2018): 354–60, https://doi.org/10.1080/02701367.2018.1481919.

4. Benjamin J. Houltberg, Kenneth T. Wang, and Sarah A. Schnitker, "Religiousness and Perceived God Perfectionism Among Elite Athletes," *Journal for the Christian Society for Kinesiology, Leisure, and Sports Studies* 4, no. 1 (2017): 29–46.

5. Ari Lamm, "Thread: Why Read the Bible in Hebrew?," *Harvest Life* (blog), February 11, 2023, https://harvest-life.org/2023/02/11/thread-why-read-the-bible-in-hebrew-by-ari-lamm/.

The Implications of Finding Your Worth in God

A few years ago, my research team asked a student, Kirsten, what moral challenge she faced. She tragically replied, "I started to hate myself. I hate it. And it comes back to that internalized homophobia. Yeah. I'm never that way towards others, because I'm like, 'Well, duh.' But if it's with me, I hear people talk about it, and I'm like, 'Oh, I hate myself. Worthless, like am I supposed to be here? Like, why am I here?' It's bad to say, but it's true. All right, if I'm going to continue to be viewed this way, like I am unnatural, then I'm worthless. God doesn't love me. He'll tolerate me. And I think that's the biggest challenge." Kirsten even received the message from other Christians that her primary meta-identity had to do with her sexual orientation versus her primary identity of her relationship to God.

Unfortunately, Kirsten is not alone. I have undertaken research with college students on a wide variety of campuses. One of the most surprising findings is how few Christian college students find their worth in God. At my own university campus, I discovered that less than a quarter of seniors found their source of worth in God. I found the same thing at other Christian institutions.[6] Why does that matter?

I have already pointed to the Bible and history, which clearly show that it matters, but I also find it helpful to examine social science research. Scholars have found that depression symptoms and suicide risk were markedly lower for students with secure (i.e., high yet noncontingent) self-esteem.[7] In other words, having a secure and stable source of worth helps one's mental health. More specifically, scholars have found that those who find their value in God have a greater sense of worth.[8] In addi-

6. Perry L. Glanzer, Jessica Martin, Elizabeth Bounds, Ted Cockle, Sarah Schnitker, and Karen Melton, "The Challenge of Finding Noncontingent, Universal Worth for Elite U.S. College Students," *Self and Identity* 23, nos. 3–4 (2024): 268–87, https://doi.org/10.1080/15298868.2024.2357848.

7. Chad E. Lakey, Jameson K. Hirsch, Lyndsay A. Nelson, and Sheri A. Nsamenang, "Effects of Contingent Self-Esteem on Depressive Symptoms and Suicidal Behavior," *Death Studies* 38, no. 9 (2014): 563–70.

8. Juelissalie Arsandaux, Ilaria Montagni, Melissa Macalli, Vincent Bouteloup, Christophe Tzourio, and Cédric Galéra, "Health Risk Behaviors and Self-Esteem Among College Students: Systematic Review of Quantitative Studies," *International Journal of Behavioral Medicine* 27, no. 2 (2020): 142–59, https://doi.org/10.1007/s12529-020-09857-w; Elizabeth M. Bounds, Julie L. Ratchford, and Sarah A. Schnitker, "Profile

tion, whether a person finds their self-worth in *God* has consistently predicted less body surveillance and more body appreciation,[9] less drug and alcohol dependence,[10] and better mental health outcomes.[11] Finding

Membership of Self-Worth Contingencies Predicts Well-Being, Virtues, and Values," *Journal of Happiness Studies* 25, no. 42 (2024), https://doi.org/10.1007/s10902-024-00758-3; Michael H. Kernis, "Toward a Conceptualization of Optimal Self-Esteem," *Psychological Inquiry* 14, no. 1 (2003): 1–26, https://doi.org/10.1207/S15327965PLI1401_01; Steven V. Rouse, "Universal Worth: Construct and Scale Development," *Journal of Personality Assessment* 94, no. 1 (2012): 62–72, https://doi.org/10.1080/00223891.2011.627960.

9. Kristin J. Homan and Tracy L. Tylka, "Development and Exploration of the Gratitude Model of Body Appreciation in Women," *Body Image* 25 (2018): 14–22, https://doi.org/10.1016/j.bodyim.2018.01.008; Jessica R. Kusina and Julie J. Exline, "Perceived Attachment to God Relates to Body Appreciation: Mediating Roles of Self-Compassion, Sanctification of the Body, and Contingencies of Self-Worth," *Mental Health, Religion & Culture* 24, no. 10 (2021): 1050–71, https://doi.org/10.1080/13674676.2021.1995345; Nicole M. Overstreet and Diane M. Quinn, "Contingencies of Self-Worth and Appearance Concerns: Do Domains of Self-Worth Matter?," *Psychology of Women Quarterly* 36, no. 3 (2012): 314–25, https://doi.org/10.1177/0361684311435221; Jaclyn A. Siegel, Katarina L. Huellemann, Courtney C. Hillier, and Lorne Campbell, "The Protective Role of Self-Compassion for Women's Positive Body Image: An Open Replication and Extension," *Body Image* 32 (2020): 136–44, https://doi.org/10.1016/j.bodyim.2019.12.003.

10. Amanda L. Giordano, Elizabeth A. Prosek, Cynthia M. Daly, Jessica M. Holm, Zachary B. Ramsey, Meagan R. Abernathy, and Kristy M. Sender, "Exploring the Relationship Between Religious Coping and Spirituality Among Three Types of Collegiate Substance Abuse," *Journal of Counseling & Development* 93, no. 1 (2015): 70–79, https://doi.org/10.1002/j.1556-6676.2015.00182.x; Jungmeen Kim and Sarah Williams, "Linking Childhood Maltreatment to Substance Use in College Students: The Mediating Role of Self-Worth Contingencies," *Journal of Aggression, Maltreatment & Trauma* 18, no. 1 (2009): 88–105, https://doi.org/10.1080/10926770802616399.

11. Bounds, "Self-Worth Contingencies"; Jennifer Crocker, "The Costs of Seeking Self–Esteem," *The Journal of Social Issues* 5, no. 3 (2002): 597–615, https://doi.org/10.1111/1540-4560.00279; Jennifer Crocker, Andrew Karpinski, Diane M. Quinn, and Sara K. Chase, "When Grades Determine Self-Worth: Consequences of Contingent Self-Worth for Male and Female Engineering and Psychology Majors," *Journal of Personality and Social Psychology* 85, no. 3 (2003): 507, https://doi.org/10.1037/0022-3514.85.3.507; Jennifer Crocker, Riia K. Luhtanen, M. Lynne Cooper, and Alexandra Bouvrette, "Contingencies of Self-Worth in College Students: Theory and Measurement," *Journal of Personality and Social Psychology* 85, no. 5 (2003): 894–908, https://doi.org/10.1037/0022-3514.85.5.894; Chad E. Lakey, Jameson K. Hirsch, Lyndsay A. Nelson, and Sheri A. Nsamenang, "Effects of Contingent Self-Esteem on Depressive Symptoms and Suicidal Behavior," *Death Studies* 38, no. 9 (2014): 563–70, https://doi.org/10.1080/07481187.2013.809035; Judy T. Sargent, Jennifer Crocker, and Riia K. Luhtanen, "Contingencies of Self–Worth and Depressive Symptoms in College

one's worth in God is not only biblically true and historically transformative; it also proves to be the best way to experience flourishing.

One understands these results when listening to Cody, who shared with me in an interview, "Well, God made me in his image and the Bible says we're like, the Greek word is *poiema*, like a poem. Like, we're—in some sense, God considers us his masterpiece and worthy of dying for, and no matter how I feel in a moment or what my external circumstances feel like, that grounding knowledge is like more self-worth than I could ever be able to give myself." Cody understands and has internalized what it means to be made in God's image.

It is important to recognize that this worth comes from God's actions toward us and not our actions toward him. For example, one student our team interviewed shared how she found worth through her relationship with God, but it was through what she did for him: "Definitely reading my Bible; praying." That is not what I am describing. We need to find our worth through God's actions toward us. In my research, I find that the students who understand this point the best often use sensory metaphors. They think about God's vision (e.g., "The value that God sees in me.") or God's words toward them (e.g., "My goal is to be defining my worth as to, 'What does God say about me?'"). This kind of thinking begins the process of internalizing how God thinks about us and our worth. Still, we must always remember that this process is continual.

The Process of Changing Your Source of Worth

Parker, a student at a Christian college, shared with us how he struggled with depression over the past year. He admitted to us that one key source of the problem was his source of worth: "I was acting as if my worth was defined by the things that I could accomplish. And if I wasn't able to keep up in my classes, or if I missed a homework assignment, or if I didn't understand a concept, I would feel that I had less value or less worth because I placed a lot of my identity in my ability to do school well."

Students," *Journal of Social and Clinical Psychology* 25, no. 6 (2006): 628–46, https://doi.org/10.1521/jscp.2006.25.6.628.

Some of this placement came from his previous success in high school: "I graduated second in my class. It wasn't that impressive really. There were only twenty or twenty-five kids. . . . But throughout my academic history, I have a history of doing well. And because I've done well in the past, there is an expectation that I will do well in the future. And that is something I began to place a lot of my identity in."

Despite this earlier success, when he came to college, he started to face a struggle: "I was still doing well, but it was harder to do well. I was having to put in a lot more effort. And I was like, 'In high school this used to be effortless. Do I have less value because I have to work harder to get the same results?' So that is functionally what I believed about my self-worth about a year ago."

Fortunately, Parker began to realize, through the mentorship of other older adults, that his misplaced source of worth was starting to influence his flourishing in life. Thus, he began to remind himself daily of the source of his worth.

> I would say that I have inherent worth as a person who is made in the image of God because God made me that way. And there is simply not anything I can do, for better or for worse that will diminish God's love for me. And what that practically looks like is even if I fail all my classes, even if I have to drop out of school, even if I have to live with my parents for the rest of my life, never get a real job that I enjoy, that I want to do that is making a difference, I just kind of bum around doing my own thing, I still have the same worth I would if I was to go on and be a doctor that cured cancer. Like the biggest loser that you can imagine, like that person has the same worth as say the most successful person on the planet. and even the most "good person" or the "worst person" that you can imagine.

Parker went on to articulate how this outlook has helped him deal with his depression—a finding that is not surprising considering the social science research I mentioned earlier.

We also must remember this truth constantly and consistently. Margot shared with our research team how she handled this process: "I think it's just like my head says the fact that I'm created by God, that I'm made in his image, that he loves me with an everlasting love . . . I think, yeah, a lot of times daily it's just the fact that he continues to walk with me in life and that he continues to show mercy to me when I turn against him in sin. I think being consistently forgiven and consistently invited into a relationship is kind of like what makes me feel valuable." Of course, this process is not always easy.

We must recognize that all of us struggle to continually shift from relying on unstable and insufficient sources of worth to God. When discussing his source of worth, Josiah shared that he fluctuated:

> What I would love to say is the answer . . . and I feel this answer a lot. But what I would love to say is the answer that I'm consistently trusting in the whole time is that I'm made in the image of God and that Jesus loves me and came to die for my sins. And I think my ultimate backbone of what I think about myself does rely on that. But in a much more sinful way, in which I fall into, I think what people think of me, friends, suitemates, new people . . . I wish I could do it perfectly of resting in what the Lord says about me. But obviously not always.

Similarly, Laura shared, "A lot of the time it's kind of bad because people's opinions and words really affect me. And if they're positive then great. Then I'm gold. But if it's like not, then that'll kind of affect me in not a good way. I wish it was more just like what the Bible says and stuff about who you are and all that stuff, but yeah, a lot of times it's mostly just what other people tell me." Both Josiah and Laura recognized that they must constantly fight the lie that their worth can be found in some other source beyond who God says they are.

Of course, we must not only recognize and fight this continual battle regarding our own worth. We must also apply this same important truth to others.

Others' Worth and Dignity in the University

As chapters 5 and 7 demonstrated, whether we see other humans as made in God's image will influence our treatment of them on many levels. I find in my research that students who understand this view show depth in their Christian maturity. They will not stoop to haze or bully other students even when their social group encourages it. They look for those on the margins and befriend them.

One of the most inspiring interviews our research team undertook was with a young gentleman faced with relating to what today would be considered one of the major outcasts on a college campus. This is the person who would be considered the leper of Jesus's time—an unclean person who should be avoided. Justin shared,

> A friend of mine whom I was close to early on at [his university], and then less so in years after that. We had been close, and then we stopped being close. And then, in the time we weren't close, he was accused of sexual misconduct. And there was a whole inquiry and all that, and pretty much every person he was close to at the time just turned against him immediately. And that's something that, usually, I would do the same thing, because they are all friends with the person who accused him. Also, it was all one group, and you side with the victim. That's what you do.

In many ways, this truth is what Christianity has taught us through Christ. Like in the story of the good Samaritan, you side with and help the victim.

Still, as Frederick Buechner reminds us, love for the victim is not always the deepest form of agape love. As Buechner wrote,

> The love for equals is a human thing—of friend for friend, brother for brother. It is to love what is loving and lovely. The world smiles. The love for the less fortunate is a beautiful thing—the love for those who suffer, for those who are poor, the sick, the failures, the unlovely. This is compassion, and it touches the heart of the world. The love for the more fortunate is a rare thing—to love those who succeed where we fail, to rejoice without envy with those who rejoice, the love of the poor for the rich, of the black man for the white man. The world is always bewildered by its saints. And then there is the love for the enemy—love for the one who does not love you but mocks, threatens, and inflicts pain. The tortured's love for the torturer. This is God's love. It conquers the world.[12]

Indeed, this love is the love that Christ showed on the cross when he cried for his torturers, "Father, forgive them, for they do not know what they are doing" (Luke 23:34).

12. Frederick Buechner, *The Magnificent Defeat* (Seabury, 1966), 105.

Justin was also faced with whether to love someone who may have tortured another person against their will. Here is how this young man responded to the accused perpetrator of this assault:

> I was not privy to the situation until he came to me and was like, "This is all going on in my life. I have no one to turn to." And I was like, "Alright, cool, I guess we're friends again." But then hearing about the story from his perspective, knowing there was another perspective also that I wasn't getting, and knowing that either someone was lying, or someone was mistaken. And there was no way to know which was the case . . . I still had to figure out: how can I love this guy who might have done something awful? I don't know. But he's still someone who's made in God's image. He's still a sinner like me, and he's asking for a listening ear. And figuring out how to do that. That was a difficult, difficult thing.

Justin, though, chose to be friends with this young man—his only friend. To love those made in God's image who have made horrific choices is the love of God.

The major temptation when dealing with an enemy is to treat them as less than human. We see it throughout history in the examples provided in chapters 5 and 7. We see this reaction from the villagers and their children in the story told by the Idiot in the introduction to part 4. We see this in genocides perpetrated in our current world, with Chinese communists placing Muslim Uyghurs in concentration camps[13] and Muslims in Syria and Nigeria seeking to exterminate Christians and Druze.

In our contemporary world, we tend to rely on the language of human rights and dignity to convince individuals, communities, and nations not to dehumanize certain groups of people and mistreat them. But this language alone is not enough. Cambridge University scholar Jeremy Waldron points out the particularly important way that relying on the image of God helps with respect for human rights:

> The foundational work that *imago Dei* does for dignity is, in my opinion, indispensable for generating the sort of strong moral constraint associated

13. Perry L. Glanzer, "The Chinese Genocide of the Uyghurs," *Christian Scholar's Review* (blog), April 28, 2021, https://christianscholars.com/ordering-our-evils-the-chinese-genocide-of-the-uyghurs/.

> with rights—and for overriding the temptation to demonize or bestialize "the worst of the worst." This temptation is so natural that it can only be answered by something that goes beyond our attitudes, even beyond "our" morality, something commanded from the depths of the pre-political and pre-social foundation of being of those we are tempted to treat in this way. *Imago Dei* presents the respect that humans as such are entitled to as something grounded, not in what we happen to care about or what humans are actually like, or more accurately, what they have been made by the Creator to be like—like unto Himself and by virtue of that likeness sacred and inviolable. We are not just clever animals, and the evil-doers among us are not just good animals gone bad: our dignity is associated with a specifically high rank in creation accorded to us by our Creator and reflecting our likeness to our Creator. Our status even as wrong-doers is to be understood in relation to this.[14]

We should not be surprised by the tribalism that exists on our campuses, in our nation, or throughout our world. Most people around the world elevate other ethnic, gender, or national sub-identities over the core identity that should be used to determine how we treat others. For Christians in particular, it should never be that "with our tongues we bless God our Father; with the same tongues we curse the very men and women he made in his image" (James 3:9 MSG). Christ has shown and called us to a better way.

14. Jeremy Waldron, "The Image of God, Rights, Reason, and Order," in *Christianity and Human Rights: An Introduction*, ed. John Witte and Frank S. Alexander (Cambridge University Press, 2010), 226.

CHAPTER NINE

Our Motivation for Bearing God's Image

Responding to God's Excellence

> "Let Us make man," said God, "to Our Image and Likeness" (Gen. 1:26). If thou awakest not at this word, O my soul; if thou art not all aflame with love of Him for His so ineffable graciousness of condescension towards thee; if thine inmost marrow burns not with longings after Him, what shall I say? Asleep shall I call thee? Or must I rather think thee dead?
>
> —Anselm, "First Meditation"[1]

Some years ago, I read back-to-back autobiographies of two retired professional tennis players who had achieved excellence during their lives: Andre Agassi and Pete Sampras. Between them, they won twenty-two Grand Slam tennis tournaments. There is little doubt that both underwent exacting forms of practice that built incredible physical and mental habits. Still, as Andre Agassi said in his autobiography, "We could not be more different, Pete and I." Sampras loved practice

1. Anselm, "First Meditation," in *Book of Meditations and Prayers*, trans. M. R. (Burns and Oates, 1872), 2.

and loved the game. Sampras shared, "I knew exactly where I wanted to go. In order to be the best player in the world, tennis has to be your life. It's a sacrifice, and something I was willing to do."[2]

In contrast, the sport of tennis tortured Agassi in ways that it never affected Sampras. On the opening page of his autobiography, Agassi writes, "I play tennis for a living, even though I hate tennis, hate it with a dark and secret passion, and always have."[3] Indeed, the hatred started early, largely driven by a domineering father who demanded excellence. Agassi recalled how he felt at age seven: "I hate tennis, hate it with all my heart, and still I keep playing, keep hitting all morning, and all afternoon, because I have no choice."[4] As Agassi's story reveals, it is possible to be outwardly excellent at a particular endeavor and inwardly hate it. You can obey rules, develop virtues, and have "good" habits without a heart for an endeavor. The same is true with life as a whole. Outwardly, you can look like you are at the top of your game, while inwardly, you can hate the game of life itself.

Habits Without the Heart

We must never confuse the practices, habits, or virtues that lead to excellence with what shapes our hearts' desires. Simply striving for and even achieving external excellence in some areas of life does not mean you love what you do. Love and excellence are two different things. If you achieve excellence merely because of your parents' wishes for you to be excellent, the money, or some other reason, when your heart is not in it, it is a tragedy.

God designed us to have hearts that long to love him and to model his excellence out of gratitude toward him. How do we get that kind of motivation and heart? Some Christians suggest that we can form and shape our heart's desires through practices that help us cultivate certain habits. For example, in his book *Desiring the Kingdom*, James

2. Fox Sports, "Sampras 'Disappointed' with Some of the Remarks in Agassi's Book," January 14, 2010, https://www.foxsports.com/stories/tennis/sampras-disappointed-by-remarks-in-agassis-book.

3. Andre Agassi, *Open: An Autobiography* (Knopf, 2009), 3.

4. Agassi, *Open*, 28.

K. A. Smith makes the argument that "habits are inscribed in our heart through bodily practices and rituals that train the heart, as it were, to desire certain ends."[5] He later reemphasizes this point by explaining, "We are selves who *are* bodies; thus the training of desire requires bodily practices in which a particular *telos* [end] is embedded."[6]

The foremost researcher on excellence, Anders Ericsson, speculates that there may be something to this idea. He muses regarding the practice needed to become excellent at some endeavor, "The practice itself may lead to physiological adaptations that produce more enjoyment and more motivation to do that activity. That is nothing but speculation at this point, but it is reasonable speculation."[7] Thus, Smith may be right about the way practices shape our hearts, although there is not enough established evidence to affirm this point.

I must admit that I have serious doubts about this claim. After all, we all encounter the limits to this view. When my colleagues and I interview students for my research, we often find it interesting that certain students will identify as "nonpracticing Catholics." Why is this the case? Consider the case of Megan and the two areas in which she underwent extensive practice for excellence.

When my colleague interviewed Megan, she was a sophomore lacrosse player for a Division 1 university and a "nonpracticing Catholic." Obviously, she had achieved excellence in one area of life. She described the sacrifice it took: "I practice probably about four to five hours a day. And you're always thinking [about it]. Like yesterday, I woke up at six a.m. and I walked over to my locker room. We had to lift, and then we had practice. The other day was conditioning, so it's a lot of mental stress and physical [stress]. I couldn't walk the whole beginning of the week because I was in so much pain." Nonetheless, she also had a different attitude toward her sacrifice than Agassi. She shared, "I love every minute of it."

She also shared the story that reveals what reinforced her love for the sport. Part of it came from the attention and glory it brings: "Throughout high school, I was very successful with what I did on the sports field and stuff. I was all over the newspaper; I was kind of the hometown hero.

5. James K. A. Smith, *Desiring the Kingdom* (Baker Academic, 2009), 58.

6. Smith, *Desiring the Kingdom*, 62.

7. Anders Ericsson and Robert Pool, *Peak: Secrets from the New Science of Expertise* (Houghton Mifflin Harcourt, 2016), 192.

I loved it; I love the attention. Yeah, and even coming here, like, I had a really good freshman year, fortunately." Although she admits, "But it wasn't the same as high school, and I think even though it was at times, but I kind of miss that attention, you know?" The hunger for attention and glory compelled her to seek excellence.

Interestingly, she also spent extensive time practicing as a Catholic when she was young, but she did not look to religion to inform her view of the good life. Her rejection of Catholic practice had nothing to do with her family background. She said, "I'm really close to my family. I was lucky, I had a very good upbringing. My sister and I, she's my best friend." Her older sister is also a devout Catholic, so she had modeled the practice. Her parents, especially her father, were overjoyed she's attending an elite Catholic university. "I think in his mind, like, he's kind of religious. His parents were super religious. They would always talk about this as the Mecca, I guess, of religious faith. It's everything they want combined into a school." She also grew up continually practicing Christian liturgies with her family. Of her parents, she said, "I mean, they used to make me go to church every Sunday. I went to CCD [Confraternity of Christian Doctrine] and did all that." This continued until high school.

Two things caused a break. First, the pursuit of excellence in athletics took the place of religious practice because "I played three sports; that's all I did." Besides athletics wooing her heart and taking her time, her learning and practice of Catholicism never wooed her heart. Indeed, she had strong words about her practice experience and her "coach": "I hated it actually. I hated CCD. The director was like an evil lady; we called her Miss Mirabella. She was awful, an awful human being. We had no idea why she was involved, and I think she was the sole reason for ruining our city's religious faith, because of her, because she was so evil. And everyone hated going, and no one cared about anything."

Today, she says, "As I've gotten older, I've kind of differentiated away from them [her family's Catholic faith] a little bit." When asked if she talked to her sister about religion, she admitted, "No. I mean, I kind of separated myself." Regarding religious beliefs, she says, "I honestly don't care. As long as no one's like harming anyone, I don't care what people really believe in spirit or religious wise. I just have my own thoughts on it and they're different than most people, I guess."

As a result, she's stopped practicing and believing the Catholic faith. She observed, "Dorm masses—it's always packed. And I always walk by and 'Eh, maybe I should?—no.' Nope, no pressure to go. Sometimes, in the back of my mind, I'll feel a little guilty not going 'cause I do pray but it's just . . . I wouldn't consider it Catholic. Like, I don't like the whole idea of the Bible, following these stories and stuff. I believe there is a higher power but not sure about everything that was written about it."

She also did not think she needed the moral community that religion provides: "But I think I have my own moral compass that is similar to that 'cause I think that's how my parents raised me. Yeah, so I think I have a good enough foundation that I don't need to refer back to a Bible to tell me what to do. And I do think there's a higher power; I do say a prayer, and I think when people die, they go to heaven. But I'm just not into that whole going to church, going somewhere to hear someone talk about something that happened so long ago." Oddly, when asked about a religious identity, though, she would still say, "I'd go with Catholic, because I've always been, like, Catholic, I guess." She says she just likes to "pick and choose" from the tradition. After all, she admits, "I can't even remember half the stuff."

So why did Megan practice so hard to be excellent in one area of life but stop practicing when it came to Catholicism? Besides the CCD teacher she disliked, one reason for this tendency in her life (and in others') is that she was raised, like Agassi, with an emphasis on certain external religious practices that failed to capture her heart. She was taught to go through the motions of Mass or CCD, but now she no longer wants to keep "practicing" since she has lost any heart or desire for it. Instead, the sports narrative, and its resulting glory and fame, captured her affections.

The Bible also warns us about engaging in religious practice without it connecting to our deeper heart's motivation. The Israelites were often excellent at following some of the rules and practices that God set up for them, but he wanted something more. The Hebrew prophets are filled with descriptions of God calling out to Israel for their hearts. For instance, as seen in Isaiah 29:13 and repeated by Jesus to the Pharisees in Matthew 15:7–9, "These people come near to me with their mouth and honor me with their lips, but their hearts are far from me. Their worship of me is based on merely human rules they have been taught."

As I mentioned in the previous chapter, God does not want us merely to obey the basic rules he provides. It also does not matter if we change the focus from rules to certain practices or habits: God first wants our hearts, our love.

The Limits of Practice

So, how does someone become motivated to love excellence in a particular area of life or in life as a whole? Not surprisingly, the excellence scholar Ericsson points out that although practice is vital to becoming an expert, it is not "inherently enjoyable."[8] As a result, he notes that practice does not nurture one's initial motivation. If we adopt an overemphasis on rules, practices, or habits, we also may place an *over*emphasis on the role of the body and the unconscious in shaping our desires and an *under*emphasis on the need for our loves, longings, and affections to be aroused and directed.

The call to engage in practice can be a call to exhaustion. After all, practice takes energy, and we can burn ourselves out (unless it is the practice of Sabbath rest). We all know of burned-out young athletes, musicians, and students raised by overly pushy moms and dads. Our introductory tennis star, Agassi, was one of them. Not surprisingly, Ericsson concludes, "Hence, interested individuals need to be engaging in the activity and motivated to improve performance before they begin deliberate practice."[9]

In other words, since practice is actually not enjoyable, someone has to be first motivated to *start* and then persist in an endeavor. Of course, Ericsson does observe that often "individuals are motivated to engage in it [practice] by its instrumental value in improving performance."[10] Still, a person must first find a reason to want to improve his or her performance. And this reason is vitally important!

8. K. Anders Ericsson, Ralf Th. Krampe, and Clemens Tesch-Romer, "The Role of Deliberate Practice in the Acquisition of Expert Performance," *Psychological Review* 100, no. 3 (1993): 363–406.

9. Ericsson, Krampe, and Tesch-Romer, "Role of Deliberate Practice," 371.

10. Ericsson, Krampe, and Tesch-Romer, "Role of Deliberate Practice," 368.

Consider a historical model, Martin Luther (1483–1546), the monk who helped start the Protestant Reformation. He engaged in an incredible amount of practice to please God and achieve excellence before him. He wanted to be the best and most righteous monk possible. He wrote, recalling his early life as a monk, "I was a good monk, and kept the rule of my order so strictly that I may say that if ever a monk got to heaven by his monkery, it was I. All my brothers in the monastery who knew me will bear me out. If I had kept on any longer, I should have killed myself with vigils, prayers, reading, and other work."[11] Luther not only thought that doing these practices would make him an excellent monk but also thought it might make him righteous in God's eyes. In other words, he engaged in all kinds of practice for the wrong reasons—to earn his salvation.

It did not work. He tried all the following to live according to the rules of his monastic "profession":

> I made a practice of confessing and reciting all my sins, but always with prior contrition; I went to confession frequently, and I performed the assigned penances faithfully. Nevertheless, my conscience could never achieve certainty but was always in doubt and said: "You have not done this correctly. You were not contrite enough. You omitted this in your confession." Therefore, the longer I tried to heal my uncertain, weak, and troubled conscience with human traditions, the more uncertain, weak, and troubled I continually made it. In this way, by observing human traditions, I transgressed them even more; and by following the righteousness of the monastic order, I was never able to reach it.[12]

Luther loved religious excellence, but while seeking to be an excellent monk, he did not yet understand the heart of the gospel revealed in the New Testament. Thus, we need to make sure that we start with a theologically informed motivation that comes from our heart's response to God's actions and then continue to allow this motivation to guide our future practice.

11. Martin Luther, as cited in Roland C. Bainton, *Here I Stand: A Life of Martin Luther* (1950; repr., Hendrickson, 2012), 26.

12. Martin Luther, *Luther's Works*, ed. Jaroslav Pelikan (Concordia, 1955), 27:13.

Love in God's Story

You do not have to teach children to love and desire prosocial or virtuous social interactions.[13] We are naturally loving human beings who desire loving actions. God made us this way. In fact, this is what the Scriptures mean when they say we are made in God's image. We naturally desire and love. The key, though, is how this desire and love are directed.

For me, in one case, it came from my earthly father. I do not remember when it started. Its beginning had no exact time that I recall. But it had a profound impact on my growing-up years. In fact, it did not end until my first week of college. I'm talking about my desire to be a professional baseball player. Long before I ever wanted to be a good person or a follower of Christ, I wanted to be excellent at baseball.

Of course, not just a baseball player in the abstract, but a great Major League Baseball player. I wanted to be part of a drama in which I could be a star. I developed this interest from my dad introducing me to this narrative. Children act out so many of these sorts of dreams from the dramas they are introduced to when they are young. My dream happened to end when I walked onto my college baseball team for one day and realized I really didn't want to pay the price. I had other desires calling for my heart.

Parents, of course, play a key role in their children's lives. They often introduce a child to a game or a practice through play. I, for example, played basketball and baseball through high school, and it likely will not surprise you that my dad's first career was being a teacher and a coach—in basketball and baseball. Many well-known athletes and musicians are excellent in their areas because their parents introduced them to these activities and served as their early coaches (Mozart, Tiger Woods, etc.).[14] From the start, relational love and admiration motivate our engagement in habits. Tiger Woods, when reflecting on why he engaged in rigorous practices to perfect his golf abilities, said, "Golf for me was

13. Alessandra Geraci, Luca Surian, Lucia Gabriella Tina, and J. Kiley Hamlin. "Human Newborns Spontaneously Attend to Prosocial Interactions," *Nature Communications* 16, no. 1 (2025), https://doi.org/10.1038/s41467-025-61517-3.

14. K. Anders Ericsson and Robert Pool, *Peak: Secrets from the New Science of Expertise* (Houghton Mifflin Harcourt, 2016).

an apparent attempt to emulate the person I looked up to more than anyone: my father."[15]

God, our Father, is the best motivator in the world. How does he motivate us? Ericsson tells us how God the Father has designed us: "While there are various ways that parents and teachers can motivate children, the motivation must ultimately be something that comes from within the child, or else it won't endure."[16] In other words, the introduction to an endeavor by parents is usually not sufficient to keep motivating a child. After all, if that were the case, my boys would have loved everything I introduced them to and had them practice as young children, including soccer, baseball, basketball, and golf. We joined and practiced all of them for a time and included coaches in our efforts. I could have pushed them to play these sports, but the example of Andre Agassi and the students I have interviewed, such as Megan, always haunts me when I think about how I am trying to shape the desires of my children and my students. I do not want them to end up hating the practice.

How do we become inspired to internalize desires or loves for something? We are introduced to a compelling drama or story. Sometimes it seems like a random introduction jump-starts this process, like going to a concert or sporting event for the first time. In the documentary *20 Feet from Stardom*, which reviews the role of backup singers in the music industry, one of the most famous backup singers recalls the spark that sent her into her career. She went to a concert, saw a backup singer, and thought, *I can do that*.[17] Similarly, a previous American gold medal skater's motivation started by watching the Olympics one winter. I wanted to be a pro baseball player because my dad took me to Major League games.

Ericsson tells the story of the Hungarian psychologist László Polgár and his Ukrainian wife, Klara. Polgár thought he knew the secret to making any child excellent in a field, and he convinced his wife to follow his plan with their three daughters. They chose chess since it has clear standards of excellence, and outstanding women chess players are rare. In the end, all three of their daughters became top-level chess players. Two of them even became grandmasters. The third daughter, Judit, became

15. David K. Wiggins, ed., *Out of the Shadows: A Biographical History of African-American Athletes* (University of Arkansas Press, 2008), 331.

16. Wiggins, *Out of the Shadows*, 189–90.

17. *20 Feet from Stardom*, directed by Moran Nelville (Radius-TWC, 2013).

a grandmaster at age fifteen and five months, the youngest expert chess master, male or female. At one point in her career, she ranked eighth in the world among all players, male or female. Overall, she held the top-ranked female position for twenty-five years!

What helped Polgár's children to become so great? Was it just their father's heavy hand? Ericsson writes, "Judit has said her father was the best motivator she has ever met. And this is perhaps the most important factor in the early days of an expert's development—maintaining that interest and motivation while the skills and habits are being built."[18] Polgár knew how to introduce his daughters to the compelling drama of chess competition.

Our hearts can be captured when we are wisely introduced to a world set within a larger story or drama. Furthermore, this narrative comes alive when we see an enticing role that we can play in that story or drama. Reading the Avengers and X-Men comic books, J. R. R. Tolkien's works (e.g., *The Hobbit*, *The Lord of the Rings*, *The Silmarillion*), Alexandre Dumas's books (e.g., *The Count of Monte Cristo*, *The Three Musketeers*), and other compelling fiction all appealed to me in this way. They caught me up in a heroic story, and as a child, I imagined myself inhabiting those worlds in heroic ways.

Although humans can create amazing stories that motivate us deeply, God's story is the greatest of all motivators. It should be no surprise, then, that he motivates us through the Scriptures by catching us up in the grandest cosmic story ever. J. R. R. Tolkien shared, "It is not difficult to imagine the peculiar excitement and joy one would feel, if any specially beautiful fairy-story were found to be 'primarily' true, its narrative to be history, without thereby necessarily losing the mythical or allegorical significance it possessed. . . . The Christian joy, the Gloria, is of the same kind. . . . But this story is supreme; and it is true."[19] God, the Great Motivator, inspires us with this true story in two ways. The problem is that Christians usually focus on only one of these ways—the great rescue.

18. Ericsson and Pool, *Peak*, 189.

19. J. R. R. Tolkien, "On Fairy Stories," ed. C. S. Lewis, *Essays Presented to Charles Williams* (Oxford University Press, 1947), 83–84.

The Great Rescue

Like Judit's father, our heavenly Father is a skilled motivator; in fact, God is the best motivator. He knows how to spur and maintain our motivation while the fruit of the Spirit is slowly being formed in our lives. To be rescued from slavery can be considered one of the greatest acts and most inspiring motivations for gratitude. Indeed, it is the motivation that God offers to both Israel and us for loving him. Consider the Ten Commandments. God does not simply drop them on the Israelites by saying, "I'm the all-powerful God, so you better follow these rules." No, he allows them to experience his miraculous story of redemption. He first saves them from brutal slavery in Egypt and then motivates them by reminding them of the wonderful narrative of rescuing them from oppression. The chapter that lists the Ten Commandments starts, "And God spoke all these words: 'I am the LORD your God, who brought you out of Egypt, out of the land of slavery'" (Exod. 20:1–2).

Imagine watching a movie in which someone saved a group of people from a hideous concentration camp and then asked them to follow some life instructions that promised to give them a better life. Then, you see the group say, "No thanks" and walk away. How would you feel about that group? You would be thinking to yourself, *They are the most ungrateful and ignorant people*. Indeed, the Israelites often wanted to go back to slavery! You may be asking yourself, *Why was this the case?* Well, often, the practice of trusting God in the wilderness to prepare them for their fight to take over the promised land became too hard. The Israelites loved different things than what God wanted.

In the New Testament, Christians are presented with this same motivation—God, through Christ, frees us from our slavery to sin. Notice that the apostles writing the New Testament epistles normally do not start with moral commands. Instead, books such as Romans, Galatians, Ephesians, Colossians, 1 Thessalonians and 2 Thessalonians, and 1 Peter and 2 Peter start with a story or a theological retelling of the meta-narrative about how God saved us through Christ.

Only after first presenting this motivation for following God's moral admonitions do the apostles then switch by citing key transition verses, such as Galatians 5:1, that lead to the first command: "It is for freedom that Christ has set us free. Stand firm, then, and do not let yourselves be burdened again by a yoke of slavery." We are motivated to follow Christ our Lord because he set us free! Or consider Romans 12:1–2: "Therefore, I urge you, brothers and sisters, *in view of God's mercy*, to offer your bodies as a living sacrifice, holy and pleasing to God—this is your true and proper worship. Do not conform to the pattern of this world, but be transformed by the renewing of your mind. Then you will be able to test and approve what God's will is—his good, pleasing and perfect will" (emphasis added). What is the motivation for living the Christian life? Our Father's mercy.

How do we learn about God's mercy? Well, we must start with the first eleven chapters of Romans. Paul uses these chapters to remind us of God's cosmic drama that will shape both our cognitive understanding and our hearts' desires. Act 1: Although created by God, we rebelled. As a result, we were all sinners who deserved death (Rom. 3:23; 6:23). Act 2: Through Christ, God saved us (Rom. 5:1; 6:23). Act 3: We are not condemned, and we have received eternal life (Rom. 5:8, 6:23). Can you think of any better story to motivate us?

The eighteenth-century minister Gilbert Nelson summed up the process simply: "For if when we were enemies, we were reconciled to God by the death of his Son; much more being reconciled, we shall be saved by his life. But seeing man receives the benefit, a reasonable care is expected from himself, and there is employment for him, to take away the rubbish of vice, and adorn the image of God with virtue."[20] Notice, however, that Nelson connects us to the first part of the story in an important way.

The First Part of the Story

Unfortunately, one of the problems with some presentations of Christian motivation is that they simply focus on salvation from slavery to sin. As Galatians 5:1 makes clear, that is an important motivation, but when left by itself, it loses one of the most important truths presented by God in the Scriptures. God saves us not simply to spend our time being grateful. He saves us for something—to fulfill the original purposes for

20. Gilbert Nelson, *The Use of Human Reason in Religion* (London, 1741), 296.

which we are created. If you miss this part of the motivation, you miss a key part of the gospel.

Our foundational moral motivation also stems from the fact that God has designed us to flourish by bearing his image through acquiring his virtues. The medieval Christian thinker Anselm captures this point clearly in a passage from his *Book of Meditations and Prayers*:

> God's Likeness, then, may be attained by us in this way; if, musing on Him as the Good, we study to be good; if, owning Him the Just, we strive to be just; if, contemplating Him the Merciful, we make endeavours after mercy. But how to His Image? Listen. God ever remembers Himself, understands Himself, loves Himself. If thou, therefore, after thy poor fashion, art unweariedly mindful of God, if thou understandest God, if thou lovest God, thou wilt then be man "to His Image"; for thou wilt be striving to do that which God does eternally. Tis the duty of man to bend his whole being to this task; the task of remembering, of understanding, and of loving the Highest Good. To this idea should every thought and every turn and folding of thy heart be moulded, chased, and formed; to be mindful of God, to understand Him, and to love Him; and thus savingly exhibit and display the dignity of thine origin in that thou wast created to the Image of God.[21]

Our motivation for moral development also emerges from our recovered understanding of our identities in relationship to God, as image bearers, children of God, and heirs of his familial blessings. It means that if these are our true identities, through the power of the Holy Spirit, we must know, love, and acquire God's virtue to become who we are made to be—image bearers of God.

Receiving the Gift of a New Identity

Anders Ericsson talks about the change in identity that happens to young people as they travel the road to excellence. He explains, "They saw themselves as 'pianists' or 'swimmers' by the age of eleven or twelve or as 'mathematicians' before they turned sixteen or seventeen."[22] In

21. Anselm, "First Meditation," 3.
22. Ericsson and Pool, *Peak*, 192.

the process of becoming excellent, they take on an important identity. However, it is important to recognize that they had to earn these identities through difficult practice.

Although God's ways of motivating us sound similar to what Ericsson described, they are even better. He does not ask us to become something we never were. Instead, he asks us to rediscover and recover *who* he originally made us to be. Moreover, we do not have to spend hours of grueling practice to adopt these identities: He gives them to us before we even start. We are new creations, children of God, and saints.

Martin Luther was transformed once he understood this story. He read (and even taught about) Romans. At first, he did not like it, particularly the verse Romans 1:17 that begins, "For in the gospel the righteousness of God is revealed . . ." Luther wrote, "I did not love, yes, I hated the righteous God who punishes sinners, and secretly, if not blasphemously, certainly murmuring greatly, I was angry with God. . . . Thus I raged with a fierce and troubled conscience." He discovered that being an excellent monk was not enough: "Though I lived as a monk without reproach, I felt that I was a sinner before God with an extremely disturbed conscience."[23]

Nevertheless, he continued to meditate on the passage, trying desperately to find out what Paul meant. Fortunately, the Holy Spirit illuminated the passage for him: "At last, by the mercy of God, meditating day and night, I gave heed to the context of the words, namely, 'In it the righteousness of God is revealed,' as it is written, 'He who through faith is righteous shall live.' There I began to understand that the righteousness of God is that by which the righteous lives by a gift of God, namely by faith."[24]

Suddenly, Luther understood that Christ is our excellence or righteousness for us. Luther's whole attitude changed: "And I extolled my sweetest word with a love as great as the hatred with which I had before hated the word 'righteousness of God.'"[25] Luther unlocked the true key to excellence. Imagine how you would want to perform for the most loving, forgiving, and gracious Father ever, who saved you from a life of

23. Martin Luther, "Preface to the Complete Edition of Luther's Latin Writings," in *Luther's Works*, vol. 34, *Career of the Reformer IV* (Concordia, 1960), 336–37.

24. Luther, "Preface to the Complete Edition of Luther's Latin Writings," 337.

25. Luther, "Preface to the Complete Edition of Luther's Latin Writings," 337.

captivity to sin by sacrificing his Son. Furthermore, God has adopted you and given you a set of new identities in Christ. We are now not only image bearers of God but also his sons and daughters (2 Cor. 6:18; Heb. 2:10; 12:8) and heirs (Rom. 8:17; Titus 3:7).

Now, once Luther understood the best theological motivation for excellence, did he stop working? Hardly. Consider the work Luther did when he understood God's grace:

> Luther's literary achievement has no parallels in the whole of human history. If that seems an extravagant claim, consider the figures. During his thirty-year public career, Luther produced 544 separate books, pamphlets, or articles, slightly more than one every three weeks. At his peak, in 1523, he managed 55. That year, 390 separate editions of his books, new and old, were published. Luther alone was responsible for over a fifth of the entire output of pamphlets by German presses during the 1520s. One scholar has totted up the totals for his rivals and supporters and concluded that the top seventeen pro-Luther pamphleteers produced 807 editions between them during the years 1518–25, whereas Luther alone produced 1,465, nearly twice as many as all the rest put together. No revolutionary leader in modern history has, without the aid of censorship or state backing, towered over a mass movement to the extent Martin Luther did.[26]

Like the apostle Paul, when Luther understood God's grace, he worked harder than the rest of them (1 Cor. 15:10).

God, by his grace, made us in his image, saved us from sin, and has given us his excellence through Christ to once again accomplish our original purpose. That should motivate us to pursue his excellence. Best of all, we once again have the ability, through the power of the Holy Spirit, to live out the purpose he has designed for us as his image bearers.

26. Alec Ryrie, *Protestants: The Faith That Made the Modern World* (Viking, 2018), 22–23.

CHAPTER TEN

The Image of God and Our Purpose

Identity Excellence

> But the meaning of this Image of God seems to be this: That as all Excellency comes from that most Excellent Author of all Beings; in whom all Excellencies are lodged formally, or essentially, or virtually; so this Excellent Author did these things in relation to Human Nature: 1. He gave him a capacity greater than any other visible, single, created Being to receive the noblest Excellencies: 2. That he gave him as great a Capacity as possibly might be consistent with such a nature to receive Divine Excellencies: 3. That he filled that Capacity with all those Excellencies that he was thus capable of, saving only that of a necessary immutability in the fruition of all those Excellencies.
>
> —Matthew Hale, 1677[1]

"Yeah. I wish I could tell you exactly what my purpose is, but being eighteen, being a younger person, it's hard to define an actual purpose in my life yet." Brian, a first-year student at an elite university, admitted he had not identified his purpose in life. "I'm still discovering my interests, what I actually want to do career-wise, and I'm picking up

1. Matthew Hale, *The Primitive Origination of Mankind, Considered and Examined According to the Light of Nature* (William Godbid, 1677), 312.

new hobbies all the time. So, to define my purpose at this young age is a really hard thing to do."

Although he used his young age as a reason why he did not have a purpose, he also admitted that he was not sure that getting older would help the process. "I think I could go a long time in my life without actually knowing my purpose. . . . It's something hard to pinpoint, to say, yeah, 'This is why I'm on this earth, this is what I'm meant to do.' I'm just not—I haven't had enough experiences in my life to actually formulate a purpose, I don't think."

As a consequence, he saw himself as trying to figure out his purpose by gaining more experience. "I guess, at this point in my life, it's about self-exploration. So, I'm taking all these new opportunities and chances to experience new things, and I'm going through with them. And this has allowed me to really discover what I'm into. And from this process of self-discovery, I think I'll be able to find a purpose in life. But I'm still learning that process of self-discovery that I haven't been able to pinpoint a purpose just yet." Brian's story did not surprise me. He had not identified as being religious, and one of the clear findings from my own and others' research is that theists have more purpose than nontheists.

Moreover, if nontheists do have a purpose, those purposes are more likely to be focused on themselves.[2] For instance, Jade told us, "My main goal in life is just to be happy and enjoy doing whatever I want to do." Likewise, Ivy shared that her purpose was "just to enjoy my life as it happens." The first part of this chapter outlines why that is the case.

In the case of theists, their greater sense of purpose stems from their focus on God and others. For example, Kara shared with us, "So I'm Muslim, and I practice Islam, and we're taught that we're created to worship God first and foremost. So, I would say that's the first and main purpose. And the rest are just being figured out." In a somewhat similar vein, Ruth mentioned that her purpose is "to share the gospel with the whole world and to love your neighbor as yourself." Similarly, Sarah mentioned the same two purposes in a different order: "It's definitely

2. Perry L. Glanzer, Jonathan P. Hill, and Byron R. Johnson, *The Quest for Purpose: The Collegiate Search for a Meaningful Life* (State University of New York Press, 2017), chaps. 7 and 10.

to . . . just help people and if the situation calls for it, share the gospel with them."

In some theistic students, I also find a change occurs if they have a conversion experience. Brooklyn talked about how she acquired a new purpose once she became a Christian right before college. Previously, she had sought to climb the achievement ladder. Now she said that her purpose was "to know God better and to serve God better in the specific constraints or unique features of that place. . . . Hopefully, if the Lord allows me to be ninety on the deathbed, I know what I'm going to remember is not the grades or the prelims or the career progression, but the community that I made along the way. The relationships. But also, I think of course the relationship with the Lord, right, and with God. So, I use that word *relationships* in a very broad way. Meaning both the community, interpersonal ones, but also the faith side and the relationship through that, too."

While I hope that every Christian student has these two components of loving God and others as part of their purpose, I have found that Christian students often conceptualize their purpose in certain ways that miss the important implications of the first part of the Christian story that is connected to being made in God's image. In the second part of this chapter, I will examine how connecting our purpose to the fact that we are made in God's image helps us have a wider view of the purpose to which God calls us.

Why Theists Have More Purpose Than Atheists and Agnostics

It is helpful to start with a simple, empirical fact. One of the reasons for the decline in purpose among high schoolers has been the rise of the nones, agnostics, and atheists. Researchers consistently find that these groups have a lower sense of purpose than theists. For example, one recent survey found that only 29 percent of atheists and agnostics agreed with the statement "I feel like I have purpose in my life; my life has meaning." In contrast, 55 percent of Protestants agreed.[3]

3. Emily Ekins, *What Americans Think About Poverty, Wealth, and Work* (Cato Institute, 2019), https://www.cato.org/publications/survey-reports/what-americans-think-about-poverty-wealth-work#overview.

My own research has uncovered one obvious reason for this discrepancy. In our national study of college students, we found that nontheistic students struggle to create their purpose from scratch.[4] As Chase shared with me, "I became an atheist and it became a lot more ambiguous about, you know, what's right and wrong, what should I do with my life?" As a result, these students find that their life purpose usually becomes reduced to one area of life instead of something that integrates all the pieces. For instance, Jude shared how his purpose was reduced to his career path: "I guess I'd say my purpose is, you know, to get through college, go to med school, and go on to be a cardiothoracic surgeon has kind of been my dream for a long time."

In contrast, we found theists, and Christians in particular, think of purpose using a more complex form of two-level reasoning. They differentiate between one's larger life purpose and one's specific career calling. Brandi illustrates this two-level thinking: "I would say in terms of my education, I'm still trying to find a purpose. But I believe I have a purpose in my life separate from my education. I would say my purpose is to live a life that reflects my faith in Jesus Christ." Similarly, Jake noted,

> I'm here to serve God and do what he wants me to do and love other people around me in whatever situation he puts me in. . . . When I was starting college, I was a lot more like, I have to have my life planned out, I need to be a computer science major, so I can get good job right after college and I was very like, wanting to be able to control things. . . . I think now I'm a lot more just accepting. I can have plans, but God also has things that he wants me to do that might be different from what I expect. . . . I'm more comfortable not knowing exactly what I'm going to be doing next in life.

In this respect, Christianity allows students to have a clear overall life purpose even when other aspects of their life, such as their future major or career, are still undecided. Having this kind of meta-purpose provides one with stability while searching for their particular career.

4. Glanzer, Hill, and Johnson, *Quest for Purpose*.

The Difference Between Self-Oriented Purposes and the Virtue of Purpose

Even when college students claim to have a purpose, however, the purpose does not always fit into what scholars call the virtue of purpose. To have the virtue of purpose, ethicists and positive psychologists insist that one must demonstrate "a stable and generalized intention to accomplish something that is at once meaningful to the self and of consequence to the world beyond the self."[5] In other words, to claim one's purpose is to be happy, experience life to the fullest, or be comfortable does not meet the criteria for having the virtue of purpose.

This distinction is important because scholars find that individuals with beyond-the-self-oriented purposes also have numerous other positive characteristics, such as physical and mental health and academic and professional success.[6] We found this recognition in an Ivy League student named Rachel. She shared with us, "Getting a good education was always to make a better income, to live a more comfortable life, but then I find that that's kind of boring. It's not fulfilling, so then like what's the point in that? . . . So, I'm obsessed with the idea that my purpose in life is to help people, to do good things, you know what I mean?" Research confirms the health of Rachel's realization. When we connect our purposes to help others, it results in pro-social outcomes.[7]

5. William Damon, Jenni Menon, and Kendall Cotton Bronk, "The Development of Purpose During Adolescence," *Applied Developmental Science* 7, no. 3 (2003): 121.

6. For a review of this literature, please consult Anthony L. Burrow and Patrick L. Hill, "Purpose as a Form of Identity Capital for Positive Youth Adjustment," *Developmental Psychology* 47, no. 4 (2011): 1196; Lisa Kiang, "Deriving Daily Purpose Through Daily Events and Role Fulfillment Among Asian American Youth," *Journal of Research on Adolescence* 22, no. 1 (2012): 185–98; Kendall Cotton Bronk, Patrick L. Hill, Daniel K. Lapsley, Tasneem L. Talib, and Holmes Finch, "Purpose, Hope, and Life Satisfaction in Three Age Groups," *The Journal of Positive Psychology* 4, no. 6 (2009): 500–510; Anthony L. Burrow, Amanda C. O'Dell, and Patrick L. Hill, "Profiles of a Developmental Asset: Youth Purpose as a Context for Hope and Well-Being," *Journal of Youth and Adolescence* 39, no. 11 (2010): 1265–73; Kendall Cotton Bronk, "The Role of Purpose in Life in Healthy Identity Formation: A Grounded Model," *New Directions for Youth Development* 2011, no. 132 (2011): 31–44; Ann S. Masten, and Marie-Gabrielle Reed, "Resilience in Development," *Handbook of Positive Psychology* (2002): 74–88.

7. Stephen G. Post, *The Hidden Gifts of Helping: How the Power of Giving, Compassion, and Hope Can Get Us Through Hard Times* (Jossey-Bass, 2011); Stephen G.

In contrast, those who are isolated, self-absorbed, and narcissistic demonstrate greater tendencies to depression, abuse of alcohol or drugs, or other self-destructive behavior.[8] These findings and this example should not be a surprise for Christians, since humans are made in God's image. As a result, we are made for beyond-the-self-focused purposes. Thus, when we choose those kinds of purposes, we come alive and flourish as human beings.

Unfortunately, we found in a nationally representative Gallup Poll we commissioned that college students rated happiness as their number one purpose.[9] Often, it also served as a default view for students still searching for purpose, such as Peyton, who told us, "I don't know what my purpose per se in life is yet, but, you know, I want to be happy." In addition, of the other top six purposes participants affirmed, four were self-oriented (experience life to the fullest, achieve success in my career, maintain a comfortable standard of living, and discover new things about the world). In other words, five of the top eight purposes that college students identified did not meet the definition of the virtue of purpose.

The only three that did were "care for a family," "build lasting friendships," and "serve others." Overall, college students thought of their purpose in largely self-oriented ways. Those kinds of purposes are not the virtue of purpose and therefore miss out on the benefits of having a beyond-the-self-oriented purpose.

Interestingly, loving God finished second to last on our national survey of college students and was strongly agreed on by only 38 percent of students. The good news, however, is that Christian students demonstrate

---

Post and Jill Neimark, *Why Good Things Happen to Good People: How to Live a Longer, Healthier, Happier Life by the Simple Act of Giving* (Broadway Books, 2008).

8. Matthew T. Lee, Maria E. Pagano, Paige S. Veta, and Byron R. Johnson, "Daily Spiritual Experiences and Adolescent Treatment Response," *Alcohol Treatment Quarterly* 32, no. 2 (2014): 271–98; Michael Hallett and Byron R. Johnson, "The Resurgence of Religion in America's Prisons," *Religions* 5, no. 3 (2014): 663–83; Sung Joon Jang, Young-Il Kim, Byron R. Johnson, Clay Polson, and Buster Smith, "Structured Voluntary Youth Activities and Positive Outcomes in Adulthood: An Exploratory Study of Involvement in Scouting and Subjective Well-Being," *Sociological Focus* 47 (2014): 238–67; Maria E. Pagano, Alexander R. Wang, Brienna M. Rowles, Matthew E. Lee, and Byron R. Johnson, "Social Anxiety and Peer-Helping in Adolescent Addiction Treatment," *Alcoholism: Clinical and Experimental Research* 39, no. 5 (2015): 887–95.

9. Glanzer, Hill, and Johnson, *Quest for Purpose*.

the virtue of purpose to a greater degree than other students. In our study of national data, we found that students who rate religion as less important and attend religious services less frequently are more likely to have self-focused purposes such as being happy, comfortable, or experiencing life to the fullest. In contrast, students who rated religion as very important and attended services weekly were more likely to affirm loving God, helping others, caring for a family, and building lasting friendships as their prioritized purposes.[10]

The Ways Christians Describe Their Purpose(s) and Their Limits

Overall, Christians with a God-oriented and others-focused purpose are more likely to flourish as human beings. Still, we also found in our study that some Christian students struggle with their purpose due to certain ways they conceive and articulate it.[11] In my research team's interviews with college students about life purpose, we find Christians tend to use four kinds of theological language. Although there are good things that can be said about each of the four ways of articulating their purpose, all four approaches also create some challenges. The first three kinds of language are used to describe their broad purpose. The last set phrase is almost always associated with their anticipated major or profession.

1. Glorify God

Due to the popular use of the 1646 Westminster Shorter Catechism, the most common language we hear from Christian students when they describe their purpose is like this line from Taylor, "To glorify God with everything I do and say." Taylor echoes the Shorter Catechism answer to the question that starts the catechism: "Q. 1. What is the chief end of

10. Glanzer, Hill, and Johnson, *Quest for Purpose*, 150–51.

11. An earlier version of the next portion of this chapter originally appeared in Perry L. Glanzer, "Why College Students Lack a Sense of Purpose," The Gospel Coalition, October 23, 2024, https://www.thegospelcoalition.org/blogs/evangelical-history/why-college-students-lack-a-sense-of-purpose/. Used by permission.

man? A: Man's chief end is to glorify God, and to enjoy him forever."[12] Holly provides a slightly different version: "I think while my purpose in life would be to worship God probably and yeah, I mean, that's the main purpose." Now, there are a couple of limitations with these answers, besides the fact that students usually leave off the "enjoy" part from the Westminster Catechism. Like Holly's answer, it is often interpreted narrowly, or its implications are ambiguous for students.

Unfortunately, this kind of language can obscure a key understanding of humanity related to the image of God. Students often fail to recognize that we glorify God by being and bearing his image. We do that by being excellent and acquiring God's virtues not simply in our careers but in every important sub-identity of life. Now, the most insightful students understand this point. For example, when I asked Taylor, "Any inkling yet in terms of how you think that might play out in your life?" he replied, "I don't know exactly what it will look like, but definitely following what I feel called to which is to go to college and I want to go to grad school and do research and eventually get married and I feel like that's all part of my purpose in glorifying God through those things and what I feel passionate about." In Taylor's case, glorifying God is combined with the passions and desires in his other sub-identities in life beyond his profession. I will say more about this important point in chapter 12.

2. To Know God and Make Him Known, Make Disciples

Other students employ Great Commission language. For example, Katy shared, "My church from home had this slogan that our purpose is to know God and make him known. So that is the purpose of my life." Milo shared that his purpose was to "make disciples." Similarly, Andrew shared that his purpose is "to share the gospel, whether that is explicitly through just speaking with people or through my actions and living as a Christian should, as the Bible directs us." Interestingly, he also noted, "But I'm not quite yet solid on what exactly my individual purpose, in terms of what I'm going to accomplish in life, is."

Certainly, these purposes are biblical. But these answers leave students such as Milo and Andrew with a narrow understanding of what

12. *The New-England Primer, with the Shorter Catechism* (Brynberg & Andrews, 1794), 46.

this task entails. For them, it primarily involves evangelism regarding Christ's salvific work on the cross versus calling people back to the original purposes God gave to humans in creation. This outlook may elevate missionaries and pastors to the most noble professions and lead one to consider other professions as simply ways that fund the mission of "making God known." It also may reduce one's purpose to particular actions and often involves elevating some professions over others. Students end up not thinking about how their purpose might involve all their sub-identities and not simply certain forms of evangelism.

3. Imitate Christ

The third common way of articulating someone's Christian purpose draws on the common Christian theme that one finds throughout church history: We should imitate Christ. Holly related to us, "I would 100 percent say my life purpose is just to live life like Jesus." Bea expanded the context of this imitation in some helpful ways: "I think as a Christian your main purpose is to emulate Jesus's teachings in every way that you can, including your future workspace and basic relationships that you have." Again, this articulation is clearly biblical, but even expansive expressions such as Bea's may miss certain theological essentials that make this task appear like it is something we add to our lives instead of something we were originally designed from the beginning of creation to do. Moreover, these answers do not make it clear in what ways we are to imitate Christ. We are not all called to be carpenters or single like Christ. Instead, there are ways we are to imitate Christ in all our sub-identities in life.

4. Vocation or Calling Language

Many students also tend to use vocation or calling language to talk about their purpose. For instance, Josiah shared that he was an active Christian, but when we asked him about his purpose in life, he interpreted the question simply to mean his job: "Still trying to figure that out. People be like, 'Oh, what do you want to do when you grow up?' And I'm just kind of like, "Uh, I don't know. Maybe this, maybe that. Who knows."

Most, however, would clearly differentiate between a professional purpose and a larger purpose for their lives. PJ told us, "I don't feel like I have that specific of a vocation or calling yet. But I would say my general purpose is to serve God with the gifts that he's given me." This language is often reinforced on Christian campuses where students may visit a "Calling and Career Center." One limit with this language, however, is that it reduces calling and vocation simply to one's career and not to other areas of life. As a result, it misses other key human endeavors or sub-identities that Christian thinkers such as Martin Luther understood as vocations or areas of calling (e.g., marriage, friendship, stewardship).

An Alternative Language and Image That Addresses These Limitations

Based on this research, I have concluded that Christian students, and all of us really, need a better, theologically informed language for how to describe our purpose that combines the important theological emphases these articulations contain but also addresses some of the key limitations.

I think the best way to introduce this approach is to consider this quote from Grace and how she described what her Christian purpose gave her: "It's given me a very clear, 'This is what I'm meant to do,' and that's sort of the outline, and then I color in between the lines. I think someone who didn't have that would find it a lot more confusing and intimidating to try to come up with the whole image and the colors in between." The key word here is *image*.

One of the odd things about many books written on vocation is the assumption that we must search for our purpose or calling through a difficult pilgrimage that requires deep discernment.

In reality, Christians often fail to acknowledge that we must all start by recognizing three important realities. First, we all have been given one important vocation: being and bearing God's image. *Every person's purpose is to be and to bear God's image.* Second, the reason God has saved us from sin is not simply for freedom to do anything, but to give us the freedom to fulfill our originally created design. In other words, God's actions toward us are what should motivate us to bear his image.

Third, we bear God's image by acquiring his excellencies in particular identities. This section explores these three aspects.

I have not met one college student who connected their purpose to being and bearing God's image (Gen. 1:27). If they did, it would help them recognize some things that other expressions do not provide. First, if we recognize that we are made in God's image, we realize that we do not gain our worth by doing something (e.g., making God known, imitating Christ, fulfilling a particular vocation). We have value simply in the reality that God made us.

Second, with great identity (our royal title as image bearers of God) comes great responsibility. J. Richard Middleton notes that this outlook is unique among ancient creation stories. Unlike other Mesopotamian creation stories in which humans are understood as mere playthings of the gods, the stars, or other heavenly bodies, the Genesis 1 creation story reinforces human agency. Being the image of God means that we have both certain capacities and the responsibility to fulfill them.

In other words, bearing God's image is our first vocation that is expected of all humans. Our calling and vocation are not simply to find a profession, although that may be part of our vocation or calling. For example, think about the things to which we are implicitly or explicitly called in Genesis 1. First, we are, as image bearers of God, to exist in a dependent, loving relationship with him. Second, it is quite clear that as image bearers, we are invited to imitate two of the things God is doing in Genesis 1 and 2: creating and stewarding. God tasks us with stewarding his creation, including our own bodies (Gen. 1:28–30; 2:15–16) and building human culture (e.g., inventing names, Gen. 2:19–20). In other words, we are to create and steward as God creates and stewards.[13]

Third, we are to exist in certain kinds of relationships with each other. The trinitarian God, who exists in eternal love, invented marriage so that we, united as man and woman, can exist in relationship with the eternal triune God. Also, we are to bear God's image by being an excellent man or an excellent woman. God also creates a world that allows humans to reproduce to allow extended families, friends, and communities. The

13. For various treatments of these views, see David Cairns, *The Image of God in Man* (Philosophical Library, 1953); Douglas John Hall, *Imaging God: Dominion as Stewardship* (Eerdmans, 1986); and Anthony Hoekema, *Created in God's Image* (Eerdmans, 1986).

following figure (10.1) illustrates this important set of purposes that emerge from this broader understanding of our created sub-identities in which we are to bear God's image by demonstrating his virtues.

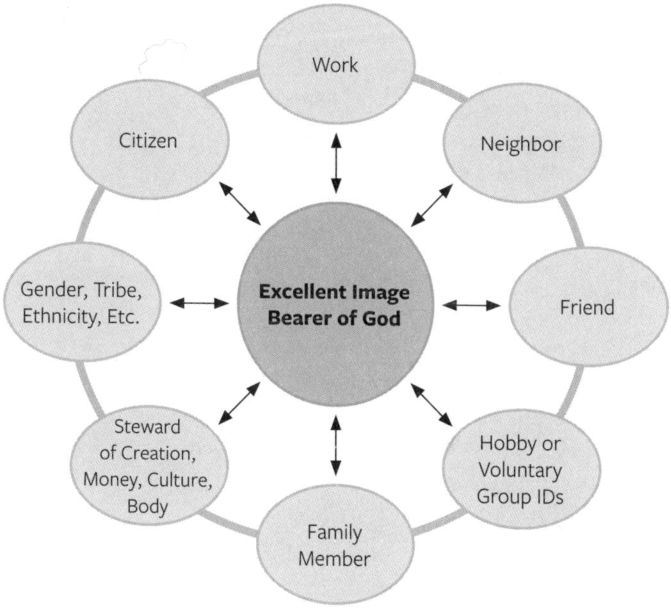

Figure 10.1. A Christian view of our central identity and related sub-identities

Our Desire for Shortcuts to Bearing God's Image

Unfortunately, since God first created Adam and Eve, human beings have wanted to take shortcuts on their way to learning to be excellent. The scholar Phillip Cary points out that Eve was not wrong to desire fruit from the Tree of Knowledge of Good and Evil. After all, Solomon's prayer for wisdom pleased God. Proverbs even commands us to "get wisdom" (Prov. 4:7). As Cary points out, the problem is that "wisdom doesn't just grow on trees, as we say. It is the fruit of a lengthy process of maturation and experience. . . . So the commandment not to eat the fruit is for our good, though it was never meant to be permanent. . . . This is the goodness that the serpent puts to the test, the work of maturation and completion that he interrupts. The ultimate perfection of creation is to be a long story."[14] Although Satan promises we can immediately "be like God," God wants us to learn his true wisdom and what it means to be an image bearer through a longer developmental process that takes time and effort. Chapter 11 discusses this process and what it means to learn how to bear God's image.

14. Phillip Cary, "The Fruit of Wisdom," *First Things*, December 12, 2013, https://www.firstthings.com/blogs/firstthoughts/2013/12/the-fruit-of-wisdom.

CHAPTER ELEVEN

The Process of Acquiring God's Virtues

For those God foreknew he also predestined to be conformed to the image of his Son.

—Romans 8:29a

But by the grace of God I am what I am, and his grace to me was not without effect. No, I worked harder than all of them—yet not I, but the grace of God that was with me.

—1 Corinthians 15:10

One of the worst-titled sports movies ever is a 1984 film called *The Natural*, starring Robert Redford. It chronicles the ups and downs of a baseball player considered to have a natural swing. While the movie itself is delightful, the title is a problem. We know from studies of excellence that no one is born a natural when it comes to sports, music, or art.[1] Indeed, the greatest stars put in the most work.

1. K. Anders Ericsson and Robert Pool, *Peak: Secrets from the New Science of Expertise* (Houghton Mifflin Harcourt, 2016).

Similarly, as a professor, I sometimes find students have a mistaken understanding of character acquisition that is similar to a misunderstanding of how people become excellent in sports, music, or a profession. They, too, assume that people are just born that way or perhaps are even born again that way. In other words, whether natural or supernatural, they think acquiring God's virtues happens with little process or work involved on the part of the individual.

Now, I am not saying that Christian conversion does not often result in incredible transformations of a person's character through the work of the Holy Spirit. It often does. But we must recognize that the lifelong journey to acquiring and sustaining God's virtues—what we were created to do—is always a long-term process. For example, if you talk to anyone who knows my wife, they would readily agree that she has an incredible talent for helping other people. It is second nature to her. Now, her desire to help did not simply come naturally. It has been honed by decades of practice in a family of four. Moreover, she grew up with an intellectually and physically disabled brother who often needed help. In addition, she had to learn to serve the family business since she grew up on a farm. She also grew up in a church that emphasized the importance of helping others as a Christian virtue. Furthermore, her professional training as a nurse and her practice as a home care nurse have refined her practice in helping others. She went through plenty of environmentally provided training opportunities to strengthen and sharpen her practice of this virtue.

Of course, after the fall, this process is even more difficult because it involves an extra step and, as always, requires God's grace and strength. Indeed, as Paul reminds us in 1 Corinthians 15, the one natural outcome we should acknowledge is that a true experience of God's grace leads us to work hard. Paul even observed that he worked harder than all the original disciples—the reason is that he had one of the deepest understandings and experiences of God's grace. He had set about making possible the murder of Christians. Yet God specifically saved him from this evil life.

We must recognize, like Paul, that life after salvation involves God-inspired arduous work and a specific process. Paul tells us of the extended three-part process in Ephesians 4:22–24: "You were taught, with regard to your former way of life, to put off your old self, which is being corrupted by its deceitful desires; to be made new in the attitude of your minds; and to put on the new self, created to be like God in true righteousness and holiness." You will see here a reference to "put off" as in reference to a self that we were originally not supposed to wear. Adam and Eve were originally supposed "to put on" God's virtues as their "clothing."

Furthermore, that end goal has not changed for us, as can be seen from Paul's instructions in Colossians 3:12–13: "Therefore, as God's chosen people, holy and dearly loved, clothe yourselves with compassion, kindness, humility, gentleness and patience. Bear with each other and forgive one another if any of you has a grievance against someone. Forgive as the Lord forgave you." In other words, in light of what God has made you, how he has chosen you, and how much he loves you, you too are supposed to learn how to "put on" or "clothe yourself" with God's virtues. Since I am now an ethics professor, I have devoted my life to studying that process. This chapter outlines what this developmental or clothing process looks like.

You Are Born Naked

We are not born clothed with God's virtues or excellences. We are born naked not only physically but also in terms of virtue—the second-nature habits that are done for the right reasons. We need parents and others to help us acquire those initial good behavioral habits. Otherwise, a child simply acts like an animal.

How do we know? We have dozens of stories of children in this state. Oxana Malaya, a young girl in Ukraine, is one of the most recent stories. Due to her neglectful parents, she was actually raised with and by dogs, so she grew up acting like a dog (including going about on her hands and feet like a dog).[2] Forming humans requires human effort. Moreover, fashioning Christ's clothing requires the effort of the human Christian community.

Therefore, Paul's reference comparing the Christian life to a fight and a race is important for helping us think about the acquisition of God's

2. "Abandoned Toddler Rescued and Raised by Feral Dogs," posted November 7, 2018, by 60 Minutes Australia, YouTube, https://www.youtube.com/watch?v=nv3ocntSSUU.

virtue. No one is simply born a great marathoner, prize fighter, or soldier. They must go through rigorous training. Indeed, the New Testament Epistles make numerous references to the importance of godly training for righteousness.

- "Everyone who competes in the games goes into strict *training*. They do it to get a crown that will not last, but we do it to get a crown that will last forever." (1 Cor. 9:25)
- "Have nothing to do with godless myths and old wives' tales; rather, *train* yourself to be godly. For physical *training* is of some value, but godliness has value for all things, holding promise for both the present life and the life to come." (1 Tim. 4:7–8)
- "All Scripture is God-breathed and is useful for teaching, rebuking, correcting and *training* in righteousness." (2 Tim. 3:16)
- "Anyone who lives on milk, being still an infant, is not acquainted with the teaching about righteousness. But solid food is for the mature, who by constant use have *trained* themselves to distinguish good from evil." (Heb. 5:13–14)
- "No discipline seems pleasant at the time, but painful. Later on, however, it produces a harvest of righteousness and peace for those who have been *trained* by it." (Heb. 12:11)

If you want to acquire God's righteousness, you have to train to acquire it.

Today, we have the privilege of benefiting from the work of researchers who have made it their life's work to study the type of training that contributes to various forms of excellence. Earlier, I mentioned Anders Ericsson and his study of excellence. What he found is not surprising for those acquainted with people who have reached a certain level of excellence.

He observed that exemplars do not simply benefit from being "born that way" or having natural ability. Instead, they go through rigorous training to develop habits, which then lead them to do excellent things as if by "second nature" (not their first nature). To give two illustrations, no one is born being able to dribble a basketball and make a shot from various distances. Instead, excellent basketball players practice this skill to make it second nature. Similarly, no one is born able to play the saxophone. One must learn how to form one's mouth and tongue and automatically play various notes as if it were second nature. This same kind of practice is required with virtues such as patience or self-control.

Ericsson also found that experts engaged in a certain kind of practice. He differentiated between three kinds of practice. One kind he identified as "naïve practice." This kind of practice is often undertaken by individuals who place an inordinate trust in repetition. To illustrate, he provided an example of an interaction between a music teacher and a student.

TEACHER: Your practice sheet says that you practice an hour a day, but your playing test was only a C. Can you explain why?

STUDENT: I don't know what happened! I could play the test last night!

TEACHER: How many times did you play it?

STUDENT: Ten or twenty.

TEACHER: How many times did you play it correctly?

STUDENT: Umm, I dunno . . . Once or twice . . .

TEACHER: Hmm . . . How did you practice it?

STUDENT: I dunno. I just played it.[3]

Simple repetition of an action does not necessarily produce excellence. After all, we can constantly repeat something poorly. That is how we develop bad habits.

The second type of practice Ericsson mentioned, "purposeful practice," is better. It consists of four ingredients: (1) well-defined goals, (2) focus, (3) feedback, and (4) pushing oneself.[4] The first element involves something such as the following from a musician: "Play the piece all the way through at the proper speed without a mistake three times in a row."[5] For a basketball player, it might be "make three hundred free throws and three-pointers a day." The same would be true with virtue-related goals. For example, perhaps you want to make it a goal not to

3. Ericsson and Pool, *Peak*, 14.
4. Ericsson and Pool, *Peak*, 15–18.
5. Ericsson and Pool, *Peak*, 15.

respond to someone who cuts you off in traffic but rather say a prayer for them, or you will help someone when you see a need, despite your busy schedule.

The second element, focus, requires that you not engage in these things in a lackadaisical manner. You must try to practice them as if you are in a concert or a game. For example, my high school basketball coach had us run sprints as a team before shooting free throws. It helped simulate how we might feel in a high-pressure game situation (especially after multiple sprints). The famous golfer Tiger Woods was known to practice putting after running multiple sprints to simulate how his body feels under pressure. The same proves true with virtue; you must learn self-control and kind answers to angry people amid such situations. I noticed that working at Chick-fil-A helped both of my sons learn this skill due to the repetitive practice of dealing with various kinds of people, including angry people.

Third, feedback is necessary to avoid bad habits. After all, one could be undertaking the practice incorrectly and therefore instilling a bad habit. That is why even the best athletes still hire coaches. They need that feedback. Christians also need that feedback from the triune God (often through the prompting and wisdom of the Spirit) and fellow believers. That is a key aspect of making disciples.

Finally, purposeful practice requires that you push yourself to get better. You are always trying to improve and reach your higher ideal. Thus, just as in sports or music one can always improve, the same is true with virtue. One's love can become deeper, one's self-control can become more precise, or one's gentleness more refined.

Deliberate Practice and Identity

Ericsson points out that there is an even higher standard of practice called deliberate practice. It involves two elements. First, "it requires a field that is already reasonably well developed—that is a field in which the best performers have attained a level of performance that clearly sets them apart from people who are just entering the field."[6] In this case,

6. Ericsson and Pool, *Peak*, 15.

he refers to things such as playing violin, chess, or baseball. In these fields, one has direct competition that helps illuminate what leads to excellence. He then claims that what does not qualify are jobs where there is not such competition, such as "business manager, teacher, electrician, engineer, and consultant."[7]

Here is where Christian understandings of excellence in life depart from Ericsson's project, but we still can draw lessons from his work. We are not in competition to be image bearers of God, and we do not have to compete to learn and understand what it means to be excellent image bearers. Instead, Christians have received this knowledge from God. It is acquired not only by the general revelation God provided to humanity through creation and humanity's thousands of years of life experience but also by God's special revelation. That's why the second element of deliberate practice is so important.

The second element of deliberate practice is that it "requires a teacher who can provide practice activities designed to help a student improve his or her performance." In other words, "Deliberate practice is purposeful practice that knows where it is going and how to get there."[8] Consequently, you cannot become excellent all on your own. You need coaches. Christians learning to be image bearers of God need both the triune God and the body of Christ to help.

This principle is exactly what Jesus taught. We need teachers (e.g., "The student is not above the teacher, nor a servant above his master. It is enough for students to be like their teachers" [Matt. 10:24–25a]). Moreover, teachers provide us with wisdom (e.g., "Therefore every teacher of the law who has become a disciple in the kingdom of heaven is like the owner of a house who brings out of his storeroom new treasures as well as old" [Matt. 13:52]). Jesus commissioned his disciples to teach others and make more disciples (Matt. 28:18–20).

Coaches or mentors often can speak from years of experience, or in the case of the triune God, from all knowledge and wisdom. They know the little things that one can and should do to become better. For instance, as I developed as a point guard in basketball, I found myself being able to predict when my teammates would make shots. It depended

7. Ericsson and Pool, *Peak*, 98.
8. Ericsson and Pool, *Peak*, 98.

on where I passed from (driving into the lane and then kicking out to a good three-point shooter was best) or my ability to make sure post players caught the ball in a place that allowed them to shoot in rhythm. As a professor, I can tell that the habits students are practicing, good or bad, are influencing their learning.

The same proves true for any practice that requires us to exercise God's virtues to achieve excellence. Think about being an excellent son or daughter, neighbor, or spouse. In marriage, one needs to learn how to love one's spouse in a way that is of particular help to them. Perhaps there are certain words or actions that one's spouse finds particularly helpful or hurtful. In all our major identities, we can learn quite a bit by the trial and error of experience, but it is even better if we can learn quickly from a teacher with years of wisdom.

You Cannot Escape Suffering

Now, it is important to know one essential thing about the nature of deliberate practice. It is hard and requires suffering. Ericsson writes, "Deliberate practice takes place outside one's comfort zone and requires a student to constantly try things that are just beyond his or her current abilities. Thus, it demands near maximal effort, which is generally not enjoyable."[9] Most movies are a curse for this reason. They do a wonderful job of inspiring our desires, sparking our passion, and moving our emotions, but they can never communicate what it really takes to be good or holy. They fail to communicate the hard work and suffering, the years of toil that must follow our inspiration. At best, those are covered in a fifteen-minute montage. The classic examples are athletic movies. They summarize in fifteen minutes and a great set of songs (picture *Rocky* or *Creed*) the long, drawn-out process that it takes to perfect the athlete, musician, or artist.

Like these processes, we must recognize that acquiring God's virtues to be excellent image bearers requires suffering. Indeed, the command to imitate Christ by joining in his suffering is found in virtually every New Testament book (Matt. 20:25–28; Mark 10:42–45; Luke 14:27–33; John

9. Ericsson and Pool, *Peak*, 99.

15:12, 20–21; Rom. 6:6–11; 1 Cor. 10:33–11:1; 2 Cor. 1:5; 4:10; Gal. 2:20; 5:24; Eph. 5:1–2; Phil. 1:29; 3:10–11; Col. 1:24; 2:20–3:1; 2 Tim. 3:12; Heb. 11:1–12:5; 1 Pet. 2:20–21; 3:14–18; 4:12–16; 1 John 2:6; 3:11–16; Rev. 12:10–11).[10] We are to be servants and experts at suffering for good. We are to die with Christ and die to ourselves. We are crucified with Christ, imitators of Christ, and therefore should engage in sacrifice to become the image bearers of God that he designed us to be.

Unfortunately, that is why plenty of people who identify as Christians do not think, desire, or act Christianly when going through life. Two recent scholars of religious emerging adults described them this way: "They want to hang on to different parts of religion that they find to be beneficial to their lives—but strictly on their terms."[11] They are spiritual babies who have avoided taking the process necessary for growth because it involves suffering. The result is that we imagine ourselves as heroes ready to suffer for the cause, but the reality is that we do not want to pay the price. The desire to be good or holy does not involve suffering like the actual process of acquiring God's virtues does.

It is helpful to recognize that we will face three distinct types of suffering during this process. These three types of suffering correspond to the three sources of evil described in the Scriptures: the flesh, the world, and the devil. As Ephesians 2:1–3 mentions, "As for you, you were dead in your transgressions and sins, in which you used to live when you followed *the ways of this world* and of *the ruler of the kingdom of the air*, the spirit who is now at work in those who are disobedient. All of us also lived among them at one time, gratifying *the cravings of our flesh* and following its desires and thoughts" (emphasis added). Following these three produces death. Of course, the good news is that "because of [God's] great love for us, God, who is rich in mercy, made us alive with Christ even when we were dead in transgressions—it is by grace you have been saved" (Eph. 2:4–5). Yet we must continue to learn to walk in this grace to be who God originally designed us to be.

Thus, deliberate Christian practice involves saying no to the cravings of our flesh. The one who teaches us how to do that is Christ, who

10. Richard Hays, *The Moral Vision of the New Testament: A Contemporary Introduction to New Testament Ethics* (HarperCollins, 1996), 27–32.

11. Melinda Lundquist Denton and Richard Flory, *Back Pocket God: Religion and Spirituality in the Lives of Emerging Adults* (Oxford University Press, 2020), 226.

became flesh but did not succumb to the fallen cravings of the flesh, whether it be turning stones to bread (Matt. 4) or the desire to have the crucifixion pass (Matt. 26:39). We, just like Christ, are sanctified through difficult trials (James 1). Think about the Israelites: God guided them to and prepared them for taking the promised land not by giving them a life of comfort but by providing them with a life that required a dependence on him for their very sustenance. Similarly, God asks us to trust and depend on him.

I remember interviewing an American widow in her seventies for my dissertation research in Vladimir, Russia. She was small and thin in stature and would remind you of your grandmother. A few years earlier, she had lost her husband of close to fifty years, who had been a pastor. At the time I interviewed her, she was living in Russia as a missionary.

Life in Russia in 1994 was difficult since the country was experiencing the breakdown of life after communism. Plus, she had to walk everywhere or take public transportation. Shopping did not involve a quick trip to the Western-style grocery store. Instead, one had to shop almost every day and haul everything home by hand. For over half the year, snow and ice covered the ground. I can still remember waiting thirty minutes for a bus in -10°F weather with the wind howling off the Volga River in that city. Just living life took a great deal of grit.

However, this older widow had not chosen to gratify her flesh by living the last days of her life playing bridge in a retirement community in Florida or Arizona. Instead, she had decided to move to Russia to suffer for the advancement of the gospel. More than other team members, her body felt the pain of life in Russia. She also faced the constant danger of falling and breaking a bone since she had to traverse snow and ice, where one fall could easily lead to a broken hip. Still, she persevered and laughed that this life reminded her of when she grew up without all the modern conveniences. I thought to myself after our interview, *I hope I am like her when I am seventy*. She was the model of someone willing to battle their flesh in the way that deliberate practice requires.

Second, in a fallen world, we can acquire these virtues only by participating in Christ's suffering. This fallen world is not kind to those who seek to bear God's image. Even ancient pagan philosophers recognized this point. I remember in college first reading in Plato's *Republic* about what Socrates thought awaited the truly just man: "[He] will be whipped;

he'll be racked; he'll be bound; he'll have both his eyes burned out; and, at the end, when he has undergone every sort of evil, he'll be crucified."[12] Christ's life shows us the truth of Socrates's prediction made over four hundred years before.

Paul's life would continue to demonstrate an endurance regarding this kind of suffering. In 2 Corinthians 11:23b–28a he describes how he worked harder than others for the gospel:

> I have worked much harder, been in prison more frequently, been flogged more severely, and been exposed to death again and again. Five times I received from the Jews the forty lashes minus one. Three times I was beaten with rods, once I was pelted with stones, three times I was shipwrecked, I spent a night and a day in the open sea, I have been constantly on the move. I have been in danger from rivers, in danger from bandits, in danger from my fellow Jews, in danger from Gentiles; in danger in the city, in danger in the country, in danger at sea; and in danger from false believers. I have labored and toiled and have often gone without sleep; I have known hunger and thirst and have often gone without food; I have been cold and naked. Besides everything else, I face daily the pressure of my concern for all the churches.

Christians must realize that fulfilling our commission both to bear God's image and to imitate Christ in a fallen world will involve suffering at the hands of others.

Third, developing God's virtue entails the suffering of spiritual warfare with demonic forces, as it did for Christ. Engaging in the spiritual warfare Paul described in Ephesians 6 or that Christ endured in Matthew 4 entails suffering. As Peter says, "Be alert and of sober mind. Your enemy the devil prowls around like a roaring lion looking for someone to devour" (1 Pet. 5:8). Fighting to avoid being devoured involves suffering.

The good news is that Christ has given us the Holy Spirit as a mentor or coach to lead us in all these situations. As Jesus tells us regarding the possibility of the second kind of suffering, "When you are brought before synagogues, rulers and authorities, do not worry about how you will defend yourselves or what you will say, for the Holy Spirit will teach you at that time what you should say" (Luke 12:11–12). Notice the coach

12. Plato, *The Republic of Plato*, trans. Alan Bloom (Basic Books, 1991), 39.

or teacher usually does not keep telling you the rules (we get these from the Bible). The coach or mentor continues to tell you specific things that help you while facing suffering, to strengthen you, to lead you toward excellence, to guide you, and to warn you.

Integrating God's Story into Our Motivation for Virtue

In light of the fact that acquiring and participating in God's virtue requires facing these three types of suffering, you need the most powerful motivation to undertake this journey toward Christian maturity. Pleasing others, following rules, and/or pursuing self-interest are not enough to take you along this arduous journey. That is not to say that taking this journey is not ultimately in your self-interest. After all, to fulfill your created telos is the definition of human flourishing. Unfortunately, many of our discussions about flourishing do not recognize that achieving this in a fallen world requires suffering.

Again, as image bearers of God, we need to look to other models to understand the most powerful God-ordained motivation for undertaking this journey. Consider Psalm 116. The writer declares,

> I love the LORD, for he heard my voice;
> he heard my cry for mercy.
> Because he turned his ear to me,
> I will call on him as long as I live. (vv. 1–2)

Later, in verses 12–14, the psalmist proclaims that his motivation for action flows from his gratitude:

> What shall I return to the LORD
> for all his goodness to me?
> I will lift up the cup of salvation
> and call on the name of the LORD.
> I will fulfill my vows to the LORD
> in the presence of all his people.

To become excellent, one must first deeply experience God's virtue, such as his love, mercy, and forgiveness. Experiencing his virtue produces a deep gratitude that motivates one to endure the pain and difficulty of Christian practice—a practice that leads us to fully bear God's image through Christ's virtue. Indeed, in a study of virtue that some colleagues and I conducted, we found that gratitude was the most important virtue or meta-virtue needed to inspire the other virtues.[13]

Developing a Moral Identity

The end result of this entire process leads one to develop what moral development scholars call a moral identity. To develop a moral identity is to internalize the standards of excellence associated with what is already objectively true. For example, one is born a son or daughter, but that does not mean one understands the objective moral standards regarding what it means to be an excellent son or daughter or that you have internalized them and adopted them beyond reasons related to mere obedience.

Parents hope that their child will develop a love and gratitude toward them that leads the child to want to be an excellent son or daughter. One also then internalizes what it means to be an excellent son or daughter so that actions associated with loving one's parents become second nature.

The same is true when it comes to moral education in a country. I remember talking to the Russian chair of the social philosophy department where I taught in Moscow for a semester. We were discussing his initial visit to the United States after the fall of the Soviet Union, when he went on a tour of Christian university campuses. He shared with me how he toured a residence hall and noticed the Christian posters up on the wall of the students' rooms. He shared amazement that such posters appeared to be there voluntarily. After enduring the forced promotion of communist propaganda throughout his life, he had a hard time imagining that college students might actually endorse Christian messaging on their own. Communism had simply failed to achieve the internalization

13. Tyler S. Greenway, Mason S. Ming, Julie L. Ratchford, Perry L. Glanzer, Kevin D. Dougherty, and Sarah A. Schnitker, "The Predictive Value of Virtue: Many Virtues Predict Lower Depression and Anxiety Symptom Scores Among College Students . . . but Gratitude Dominates," *Journal of College and Character* 25, no. 2 (2024): 140–58, https://doi.org/10.1080/2194587X.2024.2326228.

of communist ideals among the population. Of course, the free embrace of Christianity is different.

You may recognize that you are an image bearer of God, but that does not mean you understand what it entails to be an excellent image bearer or that you have internalized and practiced all that you understand. Plenty of people identify as Christians but do not think or act Christianly when going through life. Furthermore, plenty of Christians go through the motions of Christian liturgies and practice but fail to be morally transformed. What, then, is the difference between someone who internalizes Christian moral affections and thinking that leads to loving action and one who does not?

The difference is whether they have developed a moral identity. A scholar of moral identity provides a helpful summary of this concept: "The objective, the morally rational, is not imposed but rather *chosen* by the subject in the subject's freedom of will. By such free choosing the subject shapes his or her own identity, and thereby his or her own will itself, in light of objective moral reality but not in simple obedience, internalization, or socialization. . . . Moral understanding *acquires* motivational power *through its integration into the structures of the self*, into one's moral identity."[14] The person with a moral identity thus not only has internalized these moral convictions but seeks to act consistently and not betray their own sense of self. To put this point in biblical terms, one seeks not to be a hypocrite.

In particular, Christians want to build what I call a theological moral identity. In other words, we acquire certain habits of agape love, self-control, patience, and so on for theological reasons. That is not to say other moral reasons are not good ones. It is just that we know the most important audience before whom we live our moral lives is not others, or even our own conscience, but God. For example, in a recent study we undertook with college students, we asked them about a time they had practiced patience and what motivated them. Numerous students mentioned reasons that were simply pragmatic. For instance, Irene shared her moral reasoning: "I think it's because she was friends with so many of my other friends. So, I was like, 'Oh no, if I'm angry towards her, our

14. Roger Bergman, "Why Be Moral? A Conceptual Model from Developmental Psychology," *Human Development* 45 (March/April 2002): 121, emphasis original.

entire friend group is going to break up with me.' So, that's why I was so patient." That's a pragmatic, self-oriented reason versus a theological reason for being patient.

In contrast, there were those who used theological reasoning to help their patience. One student named Grace shared, "I think obviously you can't force someone to come to something. And so, I think that required some patience and knowing that God is in control. That's the thinking that helped, I think. And that God is the one that changes hearts and that will transform someone's life, not a leader nagging someone to come. Yeah. So, I think that required a bit of patience that I haven't really practiced before in that way." Like Grace, a person with a Christian moral identity is not simply acting in obedience to an external moral standard imposed on them. Instead, he or she chooses to pursue Christian excellence in a manner that demonstrates reliance on God.

Now, it should come as no surprise that scholars have found numerous benefits to developing this kind of internalized moral identity. Individuals with a developed moral identity show more care and compassion for out-groups, and they have a wider understanding of those to whom they are morally responsible.[15] They are more honest, principled, and empathetic.[16] I have also noted in another book,

> They show greater moral pleasure and elation in acts of goodness and are more willing to give time to pro-social causes. Finally, exhibiting a highly developed moral identity (and not moral reasoning) predicts positive psychological well-being and health such as higher levels of self-esteem and

15. Americus Reed II and Karl F. Aquino, "Moral Identity and the Expanding Circle of Moral Regard Toward Out-Groups," *Journal of Personality and Social Psychology* 84 (2003): 1270–86; Americus Reed II, Karl F. Aquino, and E. Levy, "Moral Identity and Judgments of Charitable Behaviors," *Journal of Marketing* 71 (2007): 178–93.

16. James R. Detert, Linda K. Trevino, and Vicki L. Sweitzer, "Moral Disengagement in Ethical Decision Making: A Study of Antecedents and Outcomes," *Journal of Applied Psychology* 93, no. 2 (2008): 374–91; Brent McFerran, Karl F. Aquino, and Michelle Duffy, "How Personality and Moral Identity Relate to Individuals' Ethical Ideology," *Business Ethics Quarterly* 30, no. 1 (2010): 35–56; Scott J. Reynolds, "Moral Attentiveness: Who Pays Attention to the Moral Aspects of Life?," *Journal of Applied Psychology* 93, no. 5 (2008): 1027–41; Scott A. Wowra, "Moral Identities, Social Anxiety, and Academic Dishonesty Among American College Students," *Ethics & Behavior* 17, no. 3 (2007): 303–21.

> lower levels of anxiety, risk behaviors and depression. Overall, a meta-analysis of 111 studies on the topic concluded that "Moral identity was found to be significantly associated with moral behavior."
>
> Study participants also revealed less negative ethical behavior. They demonstrated less unethical behavior at work and less organizational deviance. They were less likely to demean outgroups, morally disengage, rationalize harm to others, or engage in aggressive actions.
>
> In other studies of emerging adults who were considered moral exemplars, scholars discovered that the exemplars told life narratives that were more often characterized by agency themes, ideological depth, contamination sequences, redemptive experiences, and awareness of others' suffering than were the narratives of matched controls.[17]

Empirical evidence demonstrates that when you experience God's virtues and then voluntarily acquire God's virtues, as he designed you to do, you flourish. It is important to recognize, however, that this virtue acquisition must also take place within the context of our sub-identities. The next chapter explores the importance of this process.

17. Perry L. Glanzer, *Identity Excellence: A Theory of Moral Expertise for Higher Education* (Rowman & Littlefield, 2022), 43–44.

CHAPTER TWELVE

Bearing God's Image Through Excellence in Specific Sub-Identities

All excellence is proverbially difficult to attain.

—Eusebius, third and fourth century Christian historian[1]

Do you see someone skilled in their work? They will serve
before kings;
they will not serve before officials of low rank.

—Proverbs 22:29

We usually think that when someone acquires a particular character quality or excellence, such as honesty or self-control, they will continue to demonstrate that character quality in any new situation. This recognition gives us a sort of predictive power about their behavior. Thus, we spend considerable time with someone before we get married or join them in a serious business or ministry partnership. We believe we can get to know their character

1. Eusebius, *Preparation for the Gospel: Part 2*, trans. Edwin Hamilton Gifford (Baker, 1981), 491.

and that their character will be consistent later on. Perhaps not surprisingly, this belief has empirical support.[2] We find that people who are unfaithful to their spouses are also more likely to engage in professional misconduct at work.

But what if that assumption is wrong when it pertains to virtue instead of vice? Indeed, between 1928 and 1930, a group of professors researched the consistency of character traits such as honesty and self-control. They found that students who were honest or self-controlled in one situation were not always honest or self-controlled in a different situation. Thus, they concluded, "Specific actions over wide ranges of situations cannot be predicted from knowledge of conduct in one type of situation."[3]

The experiment exposed an important truth. When judging someone's character, we need to see them demonstrate virtue in more than one type of situation. It reminds me of the Sandra Bullock movie *While You Were Sleeping*, in which she judged a man's character simply by one instance of him giving up his seat on the metro for another woman. This one incident, however, did not give an accurate insight into his whole character. It turns out that he had numerous character problems.

There is also one other thing this experiment reveals, which scholars have confirmed by later experiments. We often need to learn virtues anew in specific contexts. Just as being an excellent baseball player does not make you an excellent tennis, racquetball, or pickleball player, although all involve hitting a ball, being an honest and self-controlled student does not mean that one will automatically be an honest and self-controlled friend. As scholars have found, we often must commit to and learn to practice any given virtue in new ways in each new identity context.[4] To help understand the various identity contexts in which we must learn these virtues, this chapter explores the importance of what I call identity excellence.

2. John M. Griffin, Samuel Kruger, and Gonzalo Maturana. "Personal Infidelity and Professional Conduct in 4 Settings," *Proceedings of the National Academy of Sciences* 116, no. 33 (2019): 16268–73, https://doi.org/10.1073/pnas.1905329116.

3. Hugh Hartshorne, Mark A. May, and Frank K. Shuttleworth, *Studies in the Nature of Character*, vol. 3, *Studies in the Organization of Character* (Macmillan, 1930), 375.

4. See also Richard M. Lerner and Kristina Schmid Callina, "The Study of Character Development: Towards Tests of a Relational Developmental Systems Model," *Human Development* 57, no. 6 (2015): 322–46, https://doi.org/10.1159/000368784.

The Importance of Sub-Identities

So far, we have discussed that bearing God's image involves acquiring his excellence and virtues. Indeed, it is the major way the biblical writers tell us to imitate the triune God. In this chapter, we will discuss one additional element of being and bearing God's image that is important. Just as we understand God by various sub-identities that he revealed to us (e.g., King, Warrior, Father, Potter, Teacher, Shepherd, Friend), we all have multiple sub-identities. Figure 12.1 lists some of those important sub-identities.

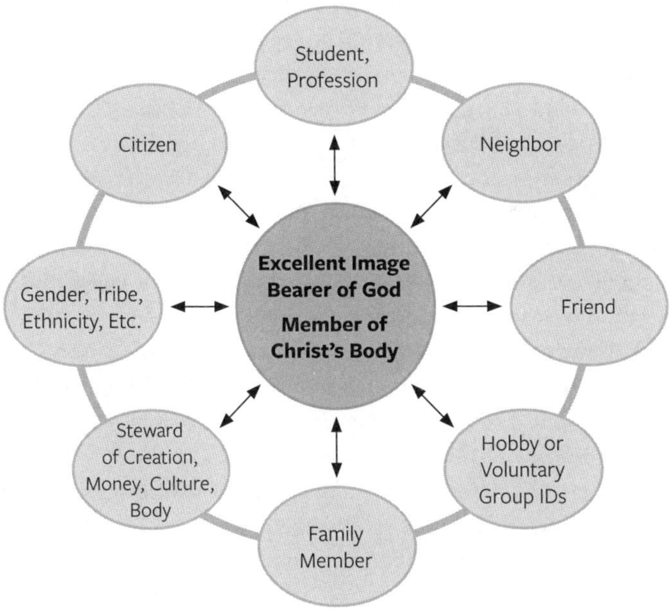

Figure 12.1. Our central identity as image bearers and our sub-identities

As mentioned, God reveals himself to us by using various human identities such as King, Lord, Father, Friend, Teacher, and Potter. Yet it is not necessarily the identities themselves that are revelatory. What is revelatory is that the triune God is our example of excellence in all these identities. Consider when Jesus describes himself as the Good

Shepherd. He makes clear that what makes the Good Shepherd exemplary is the agape love he demonstrated amid his shepherding practice: "The good shepherd lays down his life for the sheep" (John 10:11). In contrast, "The hired hand is not the shepherd and does not own the sheep. So when he sees the wolf coming, he abandons the sheep and runs away. Then the wolf attacks the flock and scatters it. The man runs away because he is a hired hand and cares nothing for the sheep" (John 10:12–13).

Interestingly, Jesus does not use a direct contrast to his observation that the hired hand "does not own the sheep," which would have him saying, "I created the sheep"—something that is true. He instead describes the intimacy he shares with the sheep and the virtue he then demonstrates in light of this loving intimacy: "I am the good shepherd; I know my sheep and my sheep know me—just as the Father knows me and I know the Father—and I lay down my life for the sheep" (John 10:14–15).

God calls us to be excellent in our sub-identities in the same way that the triune God is excellent in his. For example, God commissioned us to be stewards—stewards of nature, our own bodies, money, and our other cultural creations—and calls all of us to be excellent in these different forms of stewardship. Furthermore, simply because someone demonstrates God's virtues, such as self-control or faithfulness with the stewardship of their finances, does not automatically mean that they are self-controlled or faithful with the stewardship of their body. Now, just as God demonstrates virtue in the context of his sub-identities, we too need to learn excellence in the context of our sub-identities. We must recognize that being a gentle friend, a gentle son or daughter, and a gentle roommate—to use one example—are all different in certain ways. Therefore, we must always commit to learning how to develop and internalize God's virtues in all our different sub-identity contexts.

I discovered this reality when I made my choice about my life profession. As a high school student, I had thought deeply about what it means to be a good Christian friend, student, and steward of my body. But as I contemplated my future college major in my public high school counseling office, I remember I used an odd line of thinking. I looked for majors that had a lot of demand and made a lot of money. In other words, I thought like the pagans Christ describes in Matthew

6:32 who are consumed with food and clothing: "For the pagans run after all these things, and your heavenly Father knows that you need them." I was not guided by "seek[ing] first his kingdom and his righteousness" (v. 33).

I ended up choosing electrical engineering (a major I later changed in the first semester of college) for the wrong reasons. Instead of recognizing that God gave me certain gifts that I could use for creating things that help others (a better rationale for being an electrical engineer), I thought like a pagan while figuring out this particular sub-identity. God wants us to seek to be an excellent image bearer by being excellent in all our sub-identities.

Acquiring God's Excellence in Different Identity Contexts

Of course, Christianity shares some conception of what it means to be excellent in particular sub-identities, such as friend, spouse, or neighbor, with many worldviews developed out of God's created world. Every culture understands this point because humans all over the world have access to certain types of moral knowledge through what we call natural revelation (Rom. 1).

One of the primary ways this moral knowledge comes to them is through both human civilization and each person's conscience. As Romans 2:14–15 states, "Indeed, when Gentiles, who do not have the law, do by nature things required by the law, they are a law for themselves, even though they do not have the law. They show that the requirements of the law are written on their hearts, their consciences also bearing witness, and their thoughts sometimes accusing them and at other times even defending them."

One of the major sources of moral insight that all cultures have is that we inherit or adopt different social roles. Everyone throughout the world is a son or daughter, a citizen, a neighbor, a member of a community, and hopefully, a friend. Moreover, even if these standards have some variation from culture to culture, all cultures have moral standards about what it means to be excellent in these roles.

Furthermore, most people, and not just Christians, want to be excellent in these identities. During one research project, my team and I collected a list of over seven thousand different goals from over 2,700 college students on eight different secular and Christian campuses around the nation. Not surprisingly, most goals pertained to being excellent in something they considered their meta-identity or sub-identity.

Now, some were simply broad goals regarding excellence in a particular sub-identity. Interviewees wanted to "be a good friend to others," "be a good sister," "be a good student," "be the best wife I can be," and "take care of my body." Other goals captured different virtues necessary for excellence in a particular meta- or sub-identity. For example, concerning their relationship with God, relationships in general, their body, and being a student, some mentioned wanting to demonstrate particular virtues (see table 12.1).

Table 12.1

God	Relationships	Body	Student
"Trust the Lord's plan for my life."	"Be more patient with friends."	"Be more confident in my looks and body."	"Be a consistent student."
"Have a steady relationship with God."	"Be more present with friends and family."	"Engage in acts of self-care."	"Work hard."
"Find peace in God."	"Be a kind, supportive, and giving friend."	"Stay emotionally healthy."	"Be more open-minded."

Others made their goals even more specific. They focused on the practices that might lead to a virtue in that identity (see table 12.2).

Table 12.2

God	Relationships	Body	Student
"Think of one thing each day to thank God for."	"Spend time with friends each day."	"Eat two full healthy meals a day."	"Turn assignments in on time."
"Read the Bible and pray multiple times a day."	"Bring my friends to Christian events so they can enjoy fellowship."	"Get eight hours of sleep."	"Get homework done twenty-four hours before it's due."
"Go to church each week."	"Make one new friend."	"Workout every day."	"Wake up at least one hour before my first class."

As any scholar of goal setting would tell you, it is great to aspire to acquire a particular virtue, but it helps to develop a specific habit that will help you attain that virtue. That is what these students were doing.

Despite this moral commonality, Christianity differs from other religions and moral traditions in important ways. The next section focuses on two important differences.

The Dangers of Individualism and Communalism

Understanding ourselves as image bearers of God and members of Christ's body, while also having important sub-identities in which we train for excellence, helps us avoid two key dangers: individualism and communalism. One finds both temptations addressed when Jesus says, "If anyone comes to me and does not hate father and mother, wife and children, brothers and sisters—yes, even their own life—such a person cannot be my disciple" (Luke 14:26).

Individualism

One danger Christ identified was our tendency to love our own life before Christ. Prioritizing our individual identity apart from and above both God and community creates what we call individualism, which occurs when a person forgets that (a) we are made in God's image and thus created and defined by him and that (b) being made in God's image involves being in virtuous relationship with others through both relationally based social identities and various God-ordained institutions (e.g., families, churches, neighborhoods, countries, business, communities). Instead, an individualist imagines himself or herself as an autonomous self-author who can simply create or choose whatever other social identity he or she might desire. Individualists often downplay that we inhabit social identities gifted to us by God (e.g., man, woman, husband, wife, ethnicity), and they forget that to be fully human is to seek to exercise God's virtues in all our identities and not simply as an individual or the particular identities we choose (see figure 12.2).

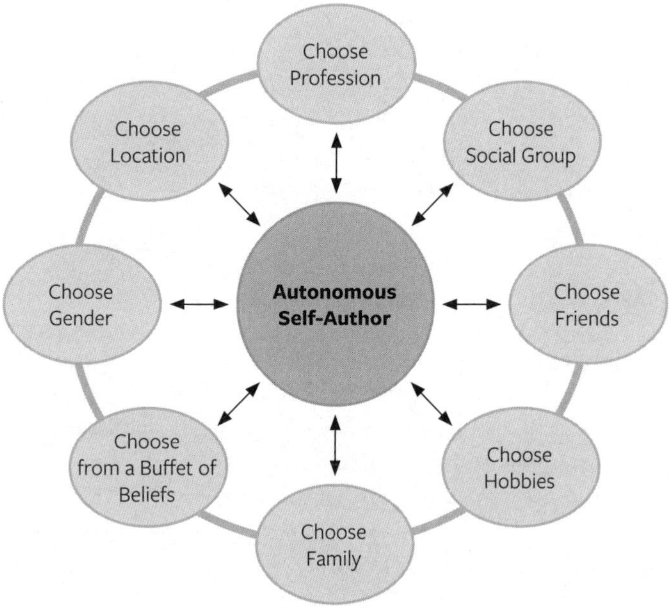

Figure 12.2. The danger of individualism

We find the celebration of the individual a particular danger within Western societies, which place a high priority on individual autonomy and individual rights. In my field of higher education, one theorist has emphasized the importance of what she called self-authorship.[5] Now, we all know that self-authorship is a good thing when it comes to children learning to go to the bathroom by themselves, dress themselves, and make the decision to clean their room for themselves. Moving forward, they need to live life without their parents hovering and checking on them. College students need to learn this kind of self-authorship.

Yet—for a variety of reasons—when I moved my son into his apartment in Dallas after he graduated from college, my prayer for him was not that he would be a total self-author. First, we should want even older adults to be sub-creators with the triune God. Jesus calls us to place our devotion and faithfulness to him first, even at the expense of our own

5. See, for example, Marcia B. Baxter Magolda, *Authoring Your Life: Developing an Internal Voice to Navigate Life's Challenges* (Stylus, 2009).

lives (e.g., Heb. 11). When it comes to a choice between saving one's own life and martyrdom, the faithful follower of God chooses martyrdom and not self-preservation.

Second, even at lower levels of commitment, we should want those around us to grow by learning how to love and care for others, to realize their need for a church community, and to recognize the importance of brothers and sisters in Christ, friends, a spouse, neighbors, and more. God did not design us for individualism or to simply be self-authors. For this reason, Christ said that a person must hate their own life (i.e., the idol of individualism) if they are to be his disciple.

Third, as the last chapter indicated, we cannot learn excellence as image bearers (or as any sub-identity) on our own. We need teachers, mentors, and models to guide us and illustrate for us what it means to be excellent in the various identities we inhabit. What does it mean to be a good aunt, an excellent son, a good citizen, an excellent husband, or a good neighbor? We need our communities to help us understand and achieve excellence in these endeavors. Yet individualists often refuse such interdependence. Despite the dangers of individualism, however, we must also recognize how relying too much on our communities can be dangerous.

Communalism

The second and opposite danger humans face is communalism. According to this view, you are nothing more than your social roles, and your individual identity must always be sacrificed for various social entities such as one's country, business, or family (see figure 12.3).

This approach was largely the one found in Jesus's time, and the practitioners of many Eastern worldviews continue to advocate for it. Within the Greek, Roman, and Confucian traditions, as described in chapter 4, you are a product of your social roles. In Christianity, however, you are an image bearer of God even without the other parts of your social context. Thus, you are responsible before God as an individual and not simply as a member of a social group. That is why Jesus noted that to follow him can even involve separation from or enmity with your "father and mother, wife and children, brothers and sisters" (Luke 14:26). These other family identities are always secondary to one's identity as

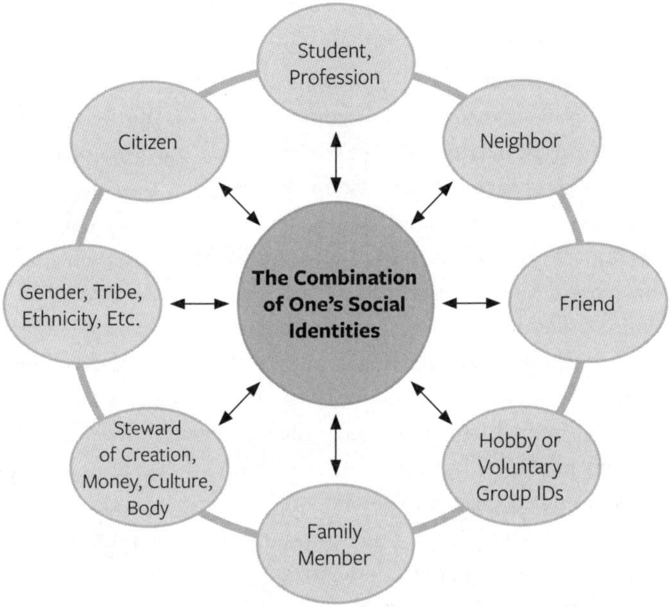

Figure 12.3. The danger of communalism

a disciple of Christ. Similarly, loyalty to one's country, ethnic or gender group, or friends should come behind one's dedication to God. One is first and foremost an image bearer of God and a member of Christ's body. If there is a community that one should be devoted to second after the triune God, it is the church.

How We Gain the Knowledge to Be Excellent in Sub-Identities

As mentioned, every identity that God has gifted us and allowed us to create has general standards of excellence. For example, all humans have received from God general moral knowledge about what it means to be an excellent friend, citizen, spouse, parent, steward of finances, and more. We do not achieve knowledge of these standards by competition, as is the case with sports, music, or other performance-based identities that rely on comparison. Instead, we obtain knowledge of excellent practice first by the general revelation provided by humanity's thousands of years of life experience engaging in these practices. Consider the stewardship of the body: Biblical writers, such as Paul, relied on readers' prior knowledge of the training that athletes go through to help Christians understand how we should train our bodies to acquire God's virtues in general.

Nonetheless, there are numerous things that general revelation does not supply. As mentioned in the previous chapters, general revelation does not provide the understanding that you are made in God's image or that even if you do not meet particular goals of excellence related to a sub-identity, you still have individual dignity and worth. Whether we reach goals we set for ourselves does not determine our value.

In addition, general revelation does not give insight into what it means to be a *Christian* friend, student, or steward of your body. For example, consider the eight virtues mentioned in chapter 4 that were demonstrated by Christ and that Jesus and the biblical writers subsequently command Christians to imitate: agape love, acceptance, forgiveness, holiness, humility, mercy, servant leadership, and enduring suffering for good. A Christian understanding of friendship, citizenship, or family life, for example, must contemplate what it means to apply these eight virtues in each sub-identity context. We must learn what it means to be a loving professional, a forgiving neighbor, a humble friend, a merciful citizen, a generous steward of money, a gentle parent, and so on. This learning is impossible in abstract forms but comes through practice that is both precise and particular. We must acquire the knowledge of and practice the unique form of virtue in each context.

Thus, we must transform this knowledge acquired by general revelation when we encounter God's special revelation in three particular ways.

Motives

In every sub-identity, we must align our motive for acquiring excellence with the best and highest motivation. In the Scriptures, we see how the Christian motivation for stewarding our body differs from pagan motivations for stewarding one's body in three important ways. We do not simply steward our bodies to feel better, live longer, or look good.

Instead, we steward our bodies because God saved us through Christ. In Romans, Paul gives the logical result that should follow in light of God's generosity: "Therefore, I urge you, brothers and sisters, in view of God's mercy, to offer your bodies as a living sacrifice, holy and pleasing to God—this is your true and proper worship" (Rom. 12:1). Christ's physical body became the instrument of our salvation. Now, we too are asked to sacrifice our bodies for God.

Moreover, because of accepting Christ's sacrifice and the gift of the Holy Spirit that Christ gave us, Paul explains to us in 1 Corinthians 6:19–20 that our bodies "are temples of the Holy Spirit, who is in you, whom you have received from God." Considering that truth, we must recognize, "You are not your own; you were bought at a price." Paul then gives the obvious ethical implication, "Therefore honor God with your bodies." The most compelling reasons for taking care of ourselves is that God created our bodies to steward, Christ sacrificed his own body to die for us, and we now house God's Spirit. Our bodies are more valuable than the greatest cathedrals ever built, and in stewarding them well, we show gratitude for Christ's sacrifice. Of course, the Old Testament temple was not just an impressive worship space but the place where the literal sacrifice of animals took place. Our body is where we sacrifice for God.

Yet we also must recognize that just as Christ rose from the dead, we will too. Earlier in that same 1 Corinthians 6 passage, Paul writes, "By his power God raised the Lord from the dead, and he will raise us also. Do you not know that your bodies are members of Christ himself?" (6:14–15a). Although, like Christ, we offer our bodies as living sacrifices, even to the point of death, we know it is not in vain since Christ rose bodily from the grave, and we will too.[6] As can be seen by these examples, we must not simply imitate, acquire, and internalize Christ's sacrificial agape love in some general way; we must learn how to apply that virtue in our specific sub-identities, such as stewards of our bodies, in biblical ways that go beyond what general revelation might teach us (e.g., taking care of your body helps you live longer).

6. For more on this topic, see Perry L. Glanzer and Austin T. Smith, eds., *Stewarding Our Bodies: A Vision for Christian Student Affairs* (Abilene Christian University Press, 2023).

The Substance of Excellence

God's revelation transforms not only our motivations but also our understanding and hopefully our affections and actions when it comes to excellence in a sub-identity. Of course, everyone has access to general revelation about what it means to be a good neighbor. State Farm even relies on this general revelation for its marketing campaign: "Like a good neighbor, State Farm is there." Of course, biblical revelation gives us more specific guidance regarding how to apply the virtue of agape love to being a good neighbor.

Consider the parable of the good Samaritan, which I would suggest medieval monks mislabeled (the label is not found in the text and was added in the Middle Ages). Instead, I would argue that we should title it the parable of the excellent neighbor. The Samaritan is simply the surprising moral exemplar of what it means to be a good neighbor. He demonstrates that an excellent neighbor shows sacrificial love not simply to someone they live near or someone within their ethnic group. Instead, they show it to any image bearer of God in need that they come across in daily life. The Samaritan is an excellent neighbor. As Jesus says of this surprising moral exemplar, "Go and do likewise" (Luke 10:37b).

Emphasizing a Virtue

The biblical writers also point out that sub-identities must sometimes emphasize a particular virtue. For instance, we find Paul giving specific instructions to husbands and wives. The apostle has already told us that all Christians should love as Christ loved (Eph. 5:1–2) and submit to one another (Eph. 5:21). Therefore, we know that husbands and wives should mutually love and submit to each other. Paul also places a special emphasis on a particular virtue for the wife (submission) and the husband (agape love) because those virtues may be particularly hard for each spouse due to the unique results of our fallen nature as men and women.

Overall, we must acknowledge that demonstrating excellence in all of our particular sub-identities involves recognizing that we must look to biblical revelation for guidance about how it should transform our motivations for excellence, the content of what it means to be excellent, and the particular virtues of God that need to be emphasized within that particular sub-identity. Figure 12.4 provides an outline of how we can envision our different sub-identities and the need to acquire virtues in each identity context. These identities are not exhaustive, but they do provide insight into what some of our major identities in life will be.[7]

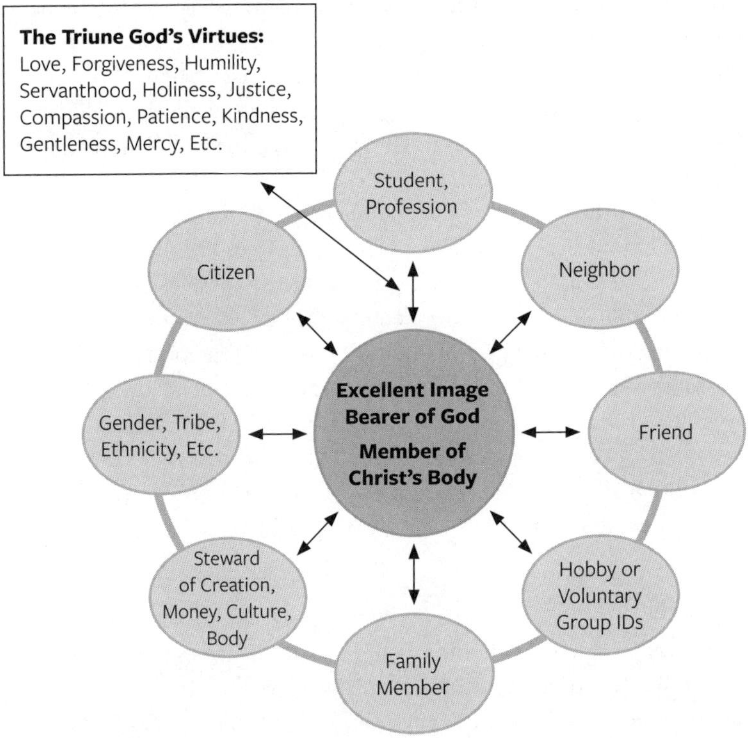

Figure 12.4. Combining excellence and virtue in all our sub-identities

Building God's Temple

As already mentioned, since the Holy Spirit lives within us, we are God's temple. Yet, like becoming the image of God, we must also finish building

7. One of the few popular Christian books I have found that takes this approach is an older volume by Seymour Van Dyken, *Becoming like Jesus: Nurturing the Virtues of Christ* (Eerdmans, 1996).

this temple. The figure above gives us some idea of what it means to build God's temple. We can also look at how God helped Israel build the original temple. Oddly, we tend to skip past these verses instead of realizing what they mean for us today. In Exodus 31:2–5, God says to Moses, "See, I have chosen Bezalel son of Uri, the son of Hur, of the tribe of Judah, and I have filled him with the Spirit of God, with wisdom, with understanding, with knowledge and with all kinds of skills—to make artistic designs for work in gold, silver and bronze, to cut and set stones, to work in wood, and to engage in all kinds of crafts."

We learn several things from this passage. We see that God filled Bezalel with his Spirit for excellence of a particular kind to contribute to the building of God's temple. Again, this kind of filling of the Spirit was not something that happened immediately. Bezalel had acquired this skill through long hours of deliberate practice.

Similarly, God fills you with his Spirit to help you continue to build God's temple, your own body, and to achieve excellence in all your identities. What will you contribute to the building of God's temple? You have something unique to offer to its design. You have something unique to offer the body of Christ as an image bearer of God, as a member of Christ's body, and in all your other sub-identities. To achieve excellence, what you offer must be informed by God's virtues. It is what we were originally designed to do.

Conclusion

As I was writing this book, a social media storm erupted around an interview with Scottie Scheffler, rated the world's number one golfer. It came from an interview answer that *Golf Digest* described as "one of the best (and deepest) press conference answers ever heard."[1] In the interview, Scheffler described his experience of and attitude toward his profession:

> I've literally worked my entire life to become good at the sport, and to have that kind of sense of accomplishment, I think, is a pretty cool feeling. You know, to get to live out your dreams is very special. . . . You know, this is not a fulfilling life. It's fulfilling from the sense of accomplishment, but it's not fulfilling from a sense of like the deepest, you know, places of your heart. You know, there are a lot of people that make it to what they thought was going to fulfill them in life. And then you get there, you get to number one in the world, and then they're like, what's the point? And, you know, I really do believe that because you know what is the point? You're like, "Why do I want to win this tournament so bad?" That's something that I wrestle with on a daily basis. It's like showing up at the Masters every year. It's like, why do I want to win this golf tournament so badly? Why do I want to win The Open Championship

1. Golf Digest (@GolfDigest), "Scottie Scheffler just gave one of the best (and deepest) press conference answers ever heard," X, June 15, 2025, https://x.com/GolfDigest/status/1945084133941649919.

> so badly? I don't know, because if I win, it's going to be awesome for about two minutes.[2]

Still, Scheffler confessed that he loved putting in the deliberate practice to be excellent in golf, but he also admitted that it did not provide his ultimate source of meaning:

> I love putting in the work. I love being able to practice. I love getting out to live out my dreams. But at the end of the day, sometimes I just don't understand the point. . . . I love the challenge. I love being able to play this game for a living. It's one of the greatest joys of my life. But does it fill the deepest, you know, wants and desires of my heart? Absolutely not. I mean I love playing golf. I love being able to compete. I love living out my dreams.[3]

Then, Scheffler pointed out that he orders his priorities differently:

> I love being a father. I love being able to take care of my son. I love being able to provide for my family out here playing golf and, you know, every day when I wake up early to go put in the work. My wife thanks me for going out and working so hard. And when I get home, I try to thank her every day for taking care of our son. . . . Family being my priority because it really is. You know, I'm blessed to be able to come out here and play golf. But if my golf ever started affecting my home life or it ever affected the relationship I have with my wife or with my son, you know that's going to be the last day that I play out here for a living. You know, this is not the be-all, end-all. This is not the most important thing in my life. And that's why I wrestle with why this is so important to me. Because you know, I would much rather be a great father than I would be a great golfer.[4]

2. Golf Digest (@GolfDigest), "Scottie Scheffler just gave one of the best (and deepest) press conference answers ever heard," X, June 15, 2025, https://x.com/GolfDigest/status/1945084133941649919.

3. Golf Digest (@GolfDigest), "Scottie Scheffler just gave one of the best (and deepest) press conference answers ever heard," X, June 15, 2025, https://x.com/GolfDigest/status/1945084133941649919.

4. Golf Digest (@GolfDigest), "Scottie Scheffler just gave one of the best (and deepest) press conference answers ever heard," X, June 15, 2025, https://x.com/GolfDigest/status/1945084133941649919.

It is rare to hear someone who has reached the top of their field share how they have done it by not placing their profession as their primary identity. It is also rare to hear someone share how they seek excellence in their whole range of sub-identities by demonstrating virtues such as gratitude.

Why the World Does Not Understand Scottie Scheffler

What was clear from the comments about this story was that many in the world cannot understand someone who would not derive their worth and purpose from their profession—especially if they were the best in the world at it. Some simply denied it. "I like Scottie but hard to believe that winning golf tournaments doesn't bring him some form of meaning and sense of desire." Others sought to diagnose him: "Haha no, he's suffering from depression. Everyone knows it's about the journey and the memories along the way. If he's in this headspace there is more going on there unfortunately" or "Damn even the #1 player in golf is depressed." One concluded, "Maybe he should retire then if he feels that way."

As I read these replies, I realized how people in the world simply do not understand two of the major themes in this book, or as one commenter shared about the responses to Scheffler's interview, "A lot of atheists exposing themselves as to why they can't understand his point." First, our worth does not come from our performance—especially our professional performance. Being number one in the world in something does not give you more worth than the lowliest person in the world (or those the world would define as the lowliest). All humans are made in God's image and are of inherent worth. Second, you cannot gain your fundamental purpose or meaning from your career or your profession. It is a sub-identity, and like any sub-identity, it cannot be the center of your identity, purpose, and world; otherwise, it becomes an idol that ultimately destroys you. Scheffler understands this point. Why is that?

What some of these people also did not know (but some commentators did) is that Scottie Scheffler is a Christian. Before trying to win the Masters golf tournament in 2022, one of the four majors, he talked about how his wife helped him calm his nerves before the final round, in which he held a three-shot lead. He shared, "I cried like a baby this morning. . . . I was so stressed out. I didn't know what to do. I was sitting there telling Meredith, 'I don't think I'm ready for this. I'm not ready, I don't feel like I'm ready for this kind of stuff,' and I just felt overwhelmed."[5]

His wife helped him place what he was doing in the Christian story. "She told me, 'Who are you to say that you are not ready? Who am I to say that I know what's best for my life?' And so, what we talked about is that God is in control and that the Lord is leading me; and if today is my time, it's my time. And if I shot 82 today, you know, somehow I was going to use it for His glory."[6] We all need someone in our lives, like Scheffler's wife, who can help reorient us to live within the Christian story even when our profession or some other sub-identity is demanding the most of us emotionally.

What Scottie Scheffler May Not Understand About Himself

Yet, as I listened to Scottie Scheffler's profound musings about life, purpose, and golf, I also wished, as a Christian, he would have made one additional and vitally important connection in answer to his question about why he strives for excellence in golf, "What is the point?" There is a deeper Christian answer to that. Being excellent in his sub-identity as a golfer is part of who he is created to be. Golf, like any form of recreation, is exactly what the word indicates. It is humans engaging in re-creation. God designed us to create in the same way that he creates. Humans created the game of golf. That creation is not meaningless. It is part of human culture that we are designed to create.

Thus, being excellent in golf, like any humanly created professional sub-identity—being a bricklayer, an accountant, a basketball player, a musician, an artist, or an engineer—is something for which God designed us as image bearers. We are also designed to be excellent at other nonprofessional sub-identities—a friend, a neighbor, a spouse or single person, a son or daughter, a father or mother, a woman or man, a citizen, and so on. We can take pleasure in fulfilling who God created us to

5. David Westin, "Scottie Scheffler Credits Wife for Grounding Him Before Final Masters Winning Round," *The Augusta Chronicle*, August 4, 2022, https://www.augustachronicle.com/story/sports/pga/2022/04/11/scottie-scheffler-credits-wife-help-before-final-masters-round/7278106001/.

6. Westin, "Scottie Scheffler Credits Wife."

be. Thus, Scheffler is absolutely right that he or anyone else should not derive their deepest sense of purpose and meaning from golf or their profession, especially in comparison to being a father or husband. He is a tremendous Christian example of how to order our priorities and our identities.

Still, I hope that we all will learn to understand our various human sub-identities in light of our most important identity. We are image bearers of God with inherent worth, a clear purpose, and a fundamental calling to bear his image by acquiring his virtues in all our sub-identities and being excellent in them. And as this book demonstrated, we cannot and should not derive our ultimate worth or purpose from any of our sub-identities. Moreover, we should not ascribe worth to others based on theirs.

Nonetheless, we should recognize that we are made to be excellent in all of our sub-identities. Indeed, Scottie Scheffler is being a great Christian example by striving for excellence not only in his professional sub-identity but also in his sub-identities as a father and husband. He wants to be excellent in fatherhood and marriage and not simply in his profession. Moreover, he has placed those more important sub-identities above being an excellent golfer. Most importantly, he recognizes that one's identity as an image bearer and child of God is what is crucial. It gives us worth and purpose and orients us amid the pressures produced by seeking to be excellent in our other sub-identities. May we all discover that reality.

Postscript for Professors, Administrators, and Student Life Staff

Although the major audience for this book is college students, I am including a postscript that addresses some specific ways that professors, administrators, and student life staff can help students be and become God's image bearers.

The Image of God and the Intrinsic Worth of Students

One of the most important applications for these groups comes from recognizing students' intrinsic worth as image bearers.

Student Affairs Staff

For a book I coauthored, *Christ-Enlivened Student Affairs*, we undertook a mixed-methods research project to understand what makes Christian student affairs unique.[1] One of the important themes we uncovered was how student affairs staff apply this theological truth. For example,

1. Perry L. Glanzer, Theodore F. Cockle, Elijah G. Jeong, and Britney N. Graber, *Christ-Enlivened Student Affairs: A Guide to Christian Thinking and Practices in the Field* (Abilene Christian University Press, 2020).

one staff member, John, shared how seeing students as made in God's image informed his work in the residence hall: "At a really fundamental level, I want students to know that God loves them, not because of what they do, but because they're created in his image. That's really significant. I find students really, I mean, we probably all struggle with that, but I see students really struggling with that. 'I'm not really sure. Does God really love me?' If you don't feel accepted in that relationship and know that it's just a grace-filled love, then it's going to be really hard."[2] John knew from working with students that some doubt their worth and God's love for them. Helping them understand and encounter that love becomes the most important first step in student affairs work.

Similarly, another staff member named Jaxon shared how this view countered some possibly dehumanizing approaches to dealing with students: "So, I think the Christian environment is unique in that because we understand that our students are created in the image of God, and that drives our interaction with them, we don't simply see them as customers, paying customers, or just a number on a spreadsheet, but as someone that God has entrusted to us. No matter what they're dealing with, there's a deeper sense of commitment to helping that student grow." For Jaxon, viewing students as made in God's image changed how he engaged in his work. As these examples illustrate, the reality that humans are made in God's image provides the key to avoiding the tendency toward dehumanizing the people whom we serve in any situation.

Numerous Christian student affairs staff noted how they especially draw on this view when dealing with three of the more controversial issues today: race, gender, and sex. For example, Grace shared how she tried to help students apply this truth with race relationships: "If you say you and I are both created in the image of God and you really mean that, and you take the time to think, *What's the impact of that? If my African American sister really is the image of God, I can't look at her the way this group of people would say you've got to look at her.*" Ruth shared how when it comes to male and female relationships, she reminded students, "We were all created in the image of God, and God created us male or female." Similarly, this theological reference also came up when

2. This quote and the following quotations in this section, unless stated otherwise, are taken from Glanzer et al., *Christ-Enlivened Student Affairs*.

asked, "How does your faith inform your response to issues related to sexuality on campus?" Numerous participants replied as follows:

- "We attempt to proactively communicate a biblical view of being created in the image of God, which includes sexuality. Many things are a departure from that ideal, not simply X or Y trending social issue."
- "The obligation we have to see the image of God in all his people and not focus exclusively on any one aspect of identity in determining our worth, our sinfulness, our ability to be part of God's body, or part of his plan."
- "Though we do not condone pornography, sex outside of marriage, or homosexual relationships, we try very sincerely to treat students engaged in these sexual practices as God's beloved children and bearers of God's image."

By viewing the students they served first and foremost as image bearers of God and not simply as members of some particular sub-group, these staff were then able to treat students with love and dignity.

Of course, they did not mean that these other sub-identities did not matter. They do, but they are not the primary identity markers we use to determine how we treat others. Michael James, a professor at Boston College, summarized their outlook the best in the student life professional context:

> A Christian anthropology for student development calls us to encounter Jesus in one another through love. As student affairs professionals . . . we are called to live a vocation that invites all members of the community to practice the "art of loving." . . . We ask ourselves, "What is the will of God in this moment, with this person?" The answer is simple: to love that person who is made in the image of God. We must initiate a love for the other right away without expecting anything in return.[3]

One student affairs staff member who mentioned this point observed that if students understand themselves as made in God's image, "they begin

3. Michael James, "A Christian Anthropology for Student Development," in *Student Life in Catholic Higher Education: Advancing Good Practice*, ed. Sandra M. Estanek (Association of Catholic Colleges and Universities, 2017), 67.

to live out this idea of seeing themselves as a creation, a creation of the Creator, and in a sense a sub-creator as well." If we bear the image of the ultimate Creator, we can help students understand and take joy in being sub-creators. For instance, creating and building a student group, starting a unique ministry, or sustaining a loving Christian community is part of being made in God's image.

Christian Professors and Administrators

I have also surveyed Christian professors across the nation about what makes their teaching Christian.[4] Many of them often referred to a core belief that one business professor shared with us: "Each learner is created in the image of God." Moreover, professors understand this belief as influencing their teaching in multiple ways. First, it shaped their views of their own responsibilities. As one psychology professor shared, she had "a belief that I have been born again by grace through Jesus Christ to reflect the image and goodness of God in a broken world and I have been endowed with intelligence, talents, and opportunities with an obligation to develop those to the fullest extent so that I may be a blessing to others guides the way I interact with my students and faculty."[5]

Second, it influenced how they understood students. One education professor shared, "I believe every student is created in the image of God with intrinsic value and worth; each has a God-given purpose in life." This understanding in turn influenced their attitude and actions. As another professor shared, "My broader Christian tradition leads me to view my students as 'divine image bearers' who are worthy of my best efforts, patience, and faith in their ability to grasp and employ effectively what I am teaching them, 'for Christ and his kingdom.'"

Finally, it informed their understanding of the divine nature of the tasks they and their students were doing in the classroom. They were not simply fulfilling a set of tasks. They were "embodying God's image and being." Thus, an English teacher shared, "We are made in his image in our creativity." One art teacher commented, "Made in the very image

4. See Perry L. Glanzer and Nathan F. Alleman, *The Outrageous Idea of Christian Teaching* (Oxford University Press, 2019).

5. This quote and the following quotations in this section are taken from Glanzer and Alleman, *Outrageous Idea*.

of God, I teach that we cannot help but reenact creation; as we do that, we embody God's image and being."

The Image of God and Collegiate General Education

One area where I have not observed this doctrine influencing Christian professors, however, pertains to how they approach general education. Think about most poorly designed general education classes in college. They tend to focus on simply giving students a broad overview of a particular subject—what I call the bag of knowledge approach. Students learn a bag of knowledge about psychology, health, English literature, public speaking, and so on. Simply teaching Introduction to Psychology, Introduction to Sociology, or Introduction to Biology does nothing to communicate to students the *aretē*, or excellence, they should pursue. Nothing in those titles indicates they involve calling students to excellence. Since students have no idea about the excellence to which a particular general education class aims, they usually find them useless and boring.

For Christians, any batch of knowledge, as 2 Peter 1 suggests, must first be framed and analyzed through faith-informed visions of excellence. Consider a general education class that focuses on being an excellent friend, citizen, steward of your finances, or steward of the environment. Having the end of excellence in mind would help you choose what knowledge to learn and what knowledge to discard. This approach does not simply leave you swimming in a sea of knowledge but rather provides an end that helps you think critically about the knowledge you need to acquire.

We do not want simply to learn about health; we want to learn how to be excellent stewards of our bodies. We do not want simply to learn political science; we want to learn what it means to be good citizens. We do not want simply to learn about religion; we want to be excellent theologians and Christians. We do not want simply to learn personal finance; we want to learn to be wise stewards of money. We must focus first on the excellence we need to acquire to know what knowledge to attain. That is why we add *aretē* to our faith before knowledge (2 Pet. 1:5). Philippians 4:8 advises Christians to think on *aretē*. To bear God's image is to meditate on his excellence and to learn how to take part in it and become excellent ourselves.

We should orient the liberal arts or general education in that direction. A batch of curricular subjects (mathematics, rhetoric, grammar, etc.) does not have the magical power to help one achieve specific forms of excellence. Instead, I argue for teaching more explicit forms of identity excellence instead of general education courses that aim to expose students to a batch of knowledge or provide some random competence.[6]

Thus, we should educate students to be excellent image bearers of God: Christians; friends; family members; citizens; men and women; stewards of the earth, our bodies, and culture; and the like. In both general education and the cocurricular domain, we need to help students supplement their faith with *aretē*/excellence. I find it interesting that "Daniel became distinguished above all the other presidents and satraps, because an excellent spirit was in him" (Dan. 6:3 RSV). We should distinguish ourselves from secular education and secular thinkers by the same spirit of excellence.

So, what might this look like in one of your courses? I encourage you to think about and explain to your students the specific excellence your courses are helping them pursue. Of course, in majors, we often imply that we are helping students achieve excellence in a professional field, but it is not always framed in that way. In contrast, I would be specific about how a class will help them be excellent historians, biologists, engineers, social workers, and so forth. For example, I think of my job as educating graduate students to be excellent higher education administrators and not simply as providing them with a collection of basic knowledge and skills that administrators need.

Overall, if you do not enter your classroom knowing, articulating, loving, and demonstrating the excellence to which you are directing students, they will see your class as merely a content dump of random information, and they will tell their friends, "I don't know how I'll be using this stuff." Let's make sure they know that we want them to acquire excellence in all facets of their lives because God has called us to his excellence. We need to engage in faith-seeking excellence (and then understanding).

6. Perry L. Glanzer, *Identity Excellence: A Theory of Moral Expertise for Higher Education* (Rowman & Littlefield, 2022).

Index